BROKEN VOWS

Divorce and the Goodness of God

John Greco
Cruciform Press | September, 2013

D1403227

This little book is decidedly not dedicated to Laurin;
such a gesture might be considered to be in poor taste.
Instead, I humbly offer this work to Jesus, the Source of
every good gift in my life, including Laurin.
May it bring him glory.

– John Greco

CruciformPress

CruciformPress.com | info@CruciformPress.com

"I really, really like this book, for it is much larger than it appears. John helps us see and live in the relentless grace and sure direction of the Father in the face of our seemingly unbearable real-life trials. He writes wisely, not from untried theory, but fire-tested experience."

Glenn T. Stanton, author, speaker, and Director of Family Formation Studies, Focus on the Family

"I've always marveled at Joseph's perspective in Genesis 50:20. He acknowledged the deep pain his brothers had inflicted on him, but also recognized God's sovereign ability to transform his personal pain into something beautiful. I had the same feeling as I read *Broken Vows*. John Greco does a beautiful job making it clear that though he never wanted his marriage to end, he would never trade the intimacy he now enjoys with his Heavenly Father. This book is filled with wisdom from cover to cover. It's the overflow of a painful personal struggle that resulted in a life full of authenticity and hope."

Phil Tuttle, President and CEO, Walk Thru the Bible

"Sadly, divorced Christians are often treated as damaged goods and second-class believers. I've felt that sting because, like John Greco, I too am a member of the Scarlet D Club. But there is good news—yes, even for the divorced—and in *Broken Vows* John shows us the gospel-based path to true forgiveness, personal healing, and life after divorce. When betrayal, rejection, and regret threatened to make John Greco a life-long victim he eventually learned to look beyond the offender to the sovereign God who never stops loving. If you've been divorced—or know a Christian who has—you need to get this book!"

Bob Bevington, co-author with Jerry Bridges of *The Bookends of the Christian Life* and *The Great Exchange*, and co-author with Joe Coffey of *Red Like Blood*

"Few are willing to share their experience of divorce in print. My friend John Greco did—and we should be thankful. This book can be helpful for those recovering from divorce, not by giving them superficial or sentimental answers to dealing with their pain, anger, and sense of abandonment, but by taking them back to the gospel truth of God's sacrificial love, absolute sovereignty, and transforming power. And it can assist those who minister to others in their broken state by alerting them to hurtful misconceptions and guiding them to biblical truths that truly help and heal. John reminds all of us—single, married, and divorced—that God should be our deepest desire, and that our greatest delight and joy is found in him alone."

William B. Barcley, Senior Pastor, Sovereign Grace Presbyterian Church, Charlotte, NC; Adjunct Professor, Reformed Theological Seminary; author of *The Secret of Contentment* and several other books and articles

"John Greco's first-hand account of coping with the trauma of broken vows offers straightforward and biblical insight into the complicated subject of Christians and divorce. *Broken Vows* provides a lifeline of hope laced with empathy, practical guidance, and non-judgmental biblical wisdom. Greco compassionately reveals how Christ can heal anyone from the devastation of divorce and how to handle those who believe otherwise."

Laura Petherbridge, speaker, and author of *When "I Do" Becomes "I Don't"* (David C. Cook)

CruciformPress
something new in Christian publishing

Our Books: Short. Clear. Concise. Helpful. Inspiring. Gospel-focused. *Print; 3 ebook formats.*

Consistent Prices: Every book costs the same.

Subscription Options: Print books or ebooks delivered to you on a set schedule, at a discount. Or buy print books or ebooks individually.

Pre-paid or Recurring Subscriptions
Print Book . . . . $6.49 each
Ebook . . . . $3.99 each

Non-Subscription Sales
1-5 Print Books . . . . $8.45 each
6-50 Print Books . . . . $7.45 each
More than 50 Print Books. . . . . $6.45 each
Single Ebooks (bit.ly/CPebks) . . . . $5.45 each
Bundles of 7 Ebooks $35.00
Ebook Distribution Program . . . . 6 pricing levels

---

Broken Vows: Divorce and the Goodness of God

Print / PDF ISBN: 978-1-936760-79-4
ePub ISBN: 978-1-936760-81-7
Mobipocket ISBN: 978-1-936760-80-0

Table of Contents

Chapters

One
A FLASH OF GOODNESS

A few years ago my marriage came crashing down around me—and I'm thankful.

I realize that doesn't sound right, so before you judge me too harshly let me explain. I wasn't glad to see my marriage end or to find out my wife had committed adultery. And I would never again want to experience the almost-unbearable pain of separation and divorce. But *I'm thankful.*

I'm thankful because, after walking through everything that's happened, I now know—in a way I simply couldn't before—that God is good.

I realize that might sound trite, like a cliché dusted off for when the world is falling apart. But that's just it—my world *was* falling apart. And there was no way I could have pretended otherwise. No Pollyanna treatment would have changed a thing, and even if I'd wanted it to, it wouldn't have fooled anyone. The only cure for my broken heart and my broken spirit was (and is) Jesus.

But I'm getting ahead of myself.

Marriage is supposed to last a lifetime, but mine didn't. My marriage ended the day my wife told me she had an affair, wasn't sorry about it, wanted a divorce, and wasn't interested in trying to salvage our relationship. Officially it took another eight months for my marriage to end on paper, but that morning as I paced through our California apartment amidst shouting, crying, praying, and doors slamming, my marriage ended. I felt broken—no longer whole—like an arm or leg had been ripped from my body. If marriage is two people becoming *one flesh*, as the Bible says, then divorce is like that flesh being torn in two without anesthetic.

A Love That Will Not Let Me Go

Seven years earlier, without shouting, crying, praying, or doors slamming, my former wife and I had a small argument while planning our wedding ceremony. I wanted to sing a hymn with our friends and family during the service. She thought that was too old-fashioned. But with the new conflict-resolution skills we'd learned in pre-marriage counseling, we came to a compromise. We decided to have a hymn sung in a contemporary style by some friends of ours as the wedding party entered the sanctuary. I chose the hymn, "O Love That Will Not Let Me Go," originally penned by George Matheson in 1882.[1]

I thought it was fitting for a wedding. Of course, the love that Matheson wrote about was God's love for his people, but love in marriage is also supposed to be a love that does not let go. It's supposed to last forever, or at least until death. That's why, when my marriage ended, I didn't know what should come next. There was never supposed to be a post-marriage period of my life. But at age thirty-four I sat on the couch in our apartment so weighed down I could barely move. With tears streaming down my face, I asked God, *Why?* with the little bit of strength I could muster.

For the next few days I made phone calls, explaining to friends and family what had happened. I tried my best to answer their questions. I cried, and I listened as each person offered an attempt at consolation, some word of advice, or a well-meaning platitude. For several nights I tossed and turned. I prayed out loud — my voice approaching a yell at times. And I did my best to sleep, but couldn't for more than a few minutes no matter what I tried. I took each moment as it came and had no expectation for the next.

The succeeding weeks brought even more changes to my life. I lost my dream job — the ministry opportunity I'd been praying about for years. My former wife and I had been set to move from California to Ohio so I could accept an associate pastor position at a church. It was the kind of church where the sweet smell of Jesus-love filled the air inside the building. Ever since my first visit it had felt like home. To some extent, I was hoping that being part of a gospel-centered community would have a healing effect on our marriage and on my wife's heart, but I never got the chance to find out. Days after my wife left, the job offer was rescinded. I listened as my would-be senior pastor and boss kindly explained that this position was probably not a good fit for me now. My heart broke a little more.

A couple of weeks after that phone call, at the end of June 2011, I did move—but not to Ohio. With no job, cash running low, and my wife unwavering in her desire to legally end our marriage, I packed up whatever personal effects I could cram into my 2002 Subaru that had no A/C and began the long, hot drive across the country—to Georgia, where most of my family lives.

As I traveled, I cried more. I prayed more. I wrestled with God more. But none of my circumstances changed. And God didn't give my aching heart any answers. He didn't tell me why things had turned out the way they did. He didn't offer me a single explanation. My identity had taken a beating. I was no longer a husband, no longer a pastor. I didn't know what the coming months and years would look like. My life had spun out of control.

On that cross-country drive, I'd sometimes wander too far from the main road in search of a meal or place to sleep. In the darkness I'd get turned around and forget how to get back to the interstate. That's how I could describe my life those days: dark, lost, and with no idea which direction would bring me home. But unlike those deserted, late-night back roads, I was never really in the dark, and I was never really lost.

When I stopped long enough to see it, there was a flickering light in the distance—a flash of divine goodness that had always been there. A flash of goodness that was not really distant after all. Jesus had never left me and had not reneged on his promise to make all things work together for my good. In my weakest moments he gave me the strength to cling to that promise—to hope that I could find a way out from under the dead weight I was carrying, to hope that my life could be made new.

When I was at my lowest, Jesus gently reminded me that nothing could separate me from his love, that my life would go on, and that I wouldn't always feel this way. When I couldn't sleep, he would bring my mind to a place of rest, to encouraging images of forgotten bits of life, times when things were more hopeful. Day by day strength returned to my spirit. Sadness and anxiety lingered on for a long time, of course—this was no quick fix—but knowing that my creator was with me made all the difference during those days.

On the third day of my drive, a familiar song came through my car's stereo speakers. "O Love That Will

Not Let Me Go," the old George Matheson hymn, being sung by Sandra McCracken—the very hymn my former wife and I had included in our wedding ceremony—but now, it struck a different chord in my heart. I thought about how my marriage had begun with promises of forever and with singing about a love that would never let me go. But now it had let me go. And I didn't feel just let go; I felt tossed away, discarded like a piece of trash.

Shortly after arriving in Georgia I stumbled upon the story behind the hymn. George Matheson had lived in Scotland during the nineteenth century. As a young man he had two passions. One was for teaching God's Word to God's people, and the other was for a young woman to whom he was engaged. Consumed by his first passion, Matheson spent his time preparing for the ministry by reading and studying voraciously. He read so many books that the strain weakened his eyes. Doctors told him the damage was irreversible and he would soon go completely blind. When his other passion learned of her fiancé's diagnosis, she called off the marriage, leaving Matheson heartbroken.

Matheson became a pastor and preacher, and later a recognized scholar, despite his blindness. He preached weekly to crowds of more than 1,500 people, none of whom he could see. It has been said his preaching was so good that most who heard him did not even realize he was blind.

But life is not without its challenges for a blind preacher. For most of his adult life, Matheson's unmarried sister Jane looked after him. She kept house, cooked meals, and helped him as he prepared his sermons. She was also a tremendous friend and companion. It was on the evening of Jane's wedding that George Matheson penned the words to "O Love That Will Not Let Me Go." The wedding scene had brought back feelings he'd experienced years earlier when he had been jilted by his beloved fiancée. And now it seemed he would be left alone once again. George's broken-heart wound was reopened, but this time he recognized a love that would never disappoint—a love that had been there all along. He felt the assurance of God's love so deeply that it took him just five minutes to pen the hymn. He later recalled that it was also the only hymn he wrote to require no editing.

When I picked out the song out for our wedding ceremony, I had no idea it had anything to do with weddings or heartbreaks. Had I known the sad story behind the hymn, I probably would have picked another. But I think Jesus knew what he was doing years earlier when he guided my mind to choose this particular song.

There is a stanza in Matheson's hymn that has become my favorite:

O Joy that seekest me through pain,
I cannot close my heart to thee;
I trace the rainbow through the rain,
And feel the promise is not vain,
That morn shall tearless be.

The rainbow in the rain—a beautiful promise displayed in the midst of a painful season—is more than just a vivid word picture. It's an allusion to Genesis 9, where God places a rainbow in the sky after the floodwaters recede. Noah stands on a patch of newly recovered dry ground, staring heavenward. He has lost much. It's time to start over, time to rebuild. And then he hears God's rainbow-promise: "Never again shall there be a flood to destroy the earth" (Genesis 9:11). But the rainbow is not just a thing of beauty; it's much weightier than that. It was a bow, as in a bow-and-arrow bow—a symbol and weapon of war. Strangely enough, the God who had just judged the world for sin with a global flood is now pointing the weapon at himself.

God's promise was an early gospel declaration. The flood had done nothing to reverse the curse. The world was still broken, the hearts of people still miserably wicked. But with that colorful war-bow in the sky, God vowed to take the punishment for sin upon himself—to deal with sin once and for all. We can now look back and see how this promise was fulfilled in

Jesus' death on the cross. The brokenness of this world has been dealt with. The pains we experience are no longer occasions for hopelessness. They are merely the remnant stings of a kingdom in decline.

The cross loudly declares that God is for us, not against us. He loves us so much that he sent his Son to die. When life grinds to a halt and it seems our worst fears have come true, we can begin to believe the lie that God is not *really* all that good or that he's not *really* in control of the universe. But the cross reminds us that God is, in fact, so good he has taken the full brunt of his own righteous anger in our place. And because of the decisive battle won at Calvary, we can have assurance that the war has already been won, the end of the story written.

Spoiler alert: God wins. Good triumphs over evil. And it's the happiest-ever-after of endings. God is still on his throne, and our stories—no matter how difficult they may be to live through—are being woven with delicate grace into the tapestry of his larger story.

When I hear "O Love That Will Not Let Me Go" today, I don't think about my wedding or broken promises or even my former wife. Instead I think about Jesus and his promise never to leave me nor forsake me. I think about the rainbow God showed to Noah. I think about what I've lost, but then I think about the gospel and the cross. I look forward to a future when God's goodness has the final word. I am filled with hope and can even look back to the darkest season of my life and see his handwriting of blessing on the wall.

Fooling Ourselves to Death

In the future there will be no need for a book like this. The very idea will seem alien. The Bible promises there will come a day when God will wipe away every tear from every eye. There will be no more mourning and no more pain. The world will be made new. Unspeakable tragedies will be redeemed. Heartache will be a distant memory. Think of the greatest pain you've suffered—it will be washed clean. I cannot explain precisely how it will happen, but God will transform and reshape your sorrow into something beautiful.

But today is not yet that day. Creation now experiences only the groans of expectation. The world that the children of God will one day inhabit has not yet been birthed. Sin and pain still leave long, foreboding shadows across the landscape. Disappointment and disaster are commonplace, breaking in and catching even the most secure among us off guard. No one is immune; no one is safe.

This, of course, is not really news. We know instinctively that this world has been broken, that things are not as they should be. We come face to face with this reality each time someone we love dies, or when we learn a friend has been diagnosed with cancer, or when we shuffle past a homeless man begging for change on the sidewalk. In the deepest parts of our being, we know how the story was supposed to go — before sin, before death, before the curse — and when we come face to face with what does not belong, we recoil or we shout against it.

We also become aware of our shattered surroundings when we experience the truly good and beautiful. We experience this in love and laughter, in good music and in delicious food. Like a bird's song echoing across the walls of a prison, it quickens a dormant longing within us for another place — a place we've never been.

But that doesn't stop us from pretending we have it all together. There is enough of life that takes place between the tragic and the sublime to fool us into believing we have not been affected by sin. Maybe it's just a coping method, a kind-of whistling past the graveyard, but we like to imagine we've discovered the secret to rise above it all. Even in churches — places that should be known as communities of grace — people often find it more tolerable to hide their pain and keep their struggles with sin and brokenness safely concealed in the darkest of closets.

If we play-act long enough we can even fool ourselves. We can begin to believe we've found a way to escape the pain, to live without the longing for things to be made right. Nothing changes in our theology of course. We still recognize that "all have sinned and fall short of the glory of God" (Romans 3:23). We still believe in the Bible, and we maintain good, solid, evangelical doctrine. But in our hearts we no longer feel the need for a Savior. We seldom ask for mercy, and repentance slips from our minds. No conscious decision is ever made to live this way, but bit-by-bit we drift away from Christ—ever so slowly, but further all the time.

It is during times like these that the greatest grace we can receive would be a shock to the heart—a jolt to defibrillate the soul and reorient it toward our first love. This is the reason I now think back on the most distressing and painful period of my life and see God's hand at work, artfully arranging sin and circumstances for my good and for his glory.

And I'm thankful.

Two
NOT WHAT I EXPECTED

"God, you are a liar."

I may not have actually uttered those words out loud, but I expressed them in the deepest recesses of my heart. I knew God's promise never to leave me or forsake me (Hebrews 13:5, Deuteronomy 31:6), but I felt alone and abandoned. My life seemed to have ground to a halt, and after months of prayer and every attempt at patience I could muster, trying to see what God might be doing with my mess of a life, I began to lose hope. It's easy to believe all things will work for good when it's someone else's life that's falling apart, but when it's your own it's hard to envision a future without the daily struggle.

Eyes to See Goodness

"And we know that for those who love God all things work together for good, for those who are called according to his purpose" (Romans 8:28).

This is a dangerous Bible verse. It has the power

to bring hope to the most tragic of circumstances. But its almost-too-good-to-be-true message also has the power to wound deeply if misunderstood or received at the wrong moment. When a child dies or life-altering medical test results are received, that's not the time to hear, "It's for the best." The thought seems cruel, jagged, and out of place. When my marriage fell apart, the idea that it was for my good made me cringe. Like a bitter-tasting herbal remedy forced down my raw throat, I couldn't keep it down. In that season my wound was too fresh for even the best of news.

There is a period after a devastating loss when a soul is unable to take in words of healing. There is a time when no words at all are welcome—only comfort. Questions fill the mind and raw emotions fill the heart. Grieving is just about the only activity on which energy can be spent. These are the moments, not to look for answers or try to find any sort of good in the situation, but to pour yourself out to Jesus. When the pain of divorce is more than you can carry, he is able to carry it. He is able to grieve with you as a brother-in-arms. He too was betrayed. He too was abandoned by those who were closest to him. He too was cast aside and rejected by those whom he loved. He is able to sympathize and console because, no matter how deep or personal the pain, he has experienced it. The passion of Jesus—his suffering and the cross—make him a worthy comforter and a wonderful friend.

But after the initial period of grief and mourning, when a person is able to step out in a quest for answers to the soul's deepest questions, it can still be difficult to accept that our unspeakable pains may be ingredients in God's good plan. I believe part of the difficulty with receiving a verse like Romans 8:28 is that without the help of the Holy Spirit, we cannot truly understand what *good* means.

When I was at a low point in my journey, looking for answers, a friend passed along a sermon by Matt Chandler, pastor of The Village Church.[2] He thought it would bring me some encouragement. It did, but it also provided me with a powerful illustration to understand what may be going on behind the scenes when we walk through a life-altering event.

In the sermon Chandler describes a horrific scenario:

> If I told you that a man knocked me unconscious, cracked open my skull and cut out my right frontal lobe, and then afterwards pumped my brain full of radiation and then poisoned me for eighteen months, you would probably ask the question "Why?"…You'd be like "Hunt that dude down!"

This is what it feels like when we encounter tragedies. We'd like to think we can avoid them, so they usually surprise us, catching us off-guard. These events can cut us deeply, leaving pain and lasting scars. And just like the listener in Chandler's illustration, we can become confused and frustrated. Without proper care, the tinge of anger and bitterness will take hold.

Chandler then goes on to say,

> But it all changes if I say…I found out why: there was a malignant form of cancer in my right frontal lobe and the only way to save my life — to extend my days — was to knock me unconscious,…cut out my right frontal lobe, [and] pump me full of radiation and poison for eighteen months….What makes things difficult here and now is that we can't see that [it's cancer].

What feels like an atrocity in this life can, in reality, be life-saving surgery.

Caught in the initial shock of a broken marriage or a similar heartache, eternal perspective can be in short supply. The pain is here and now — the life-jolt too new to be fully understood on an earthly level, let alone a heavenly one. And as the wound ages and the initial shock wears off, the pain often dulls. That is not to say the pain necessarily lessens, but only that we can get used to it. It becomes part of us, and we may begin to forget what life was like before the tragedy. The idea that God could be using heartbreaking moments for our good becomes a nice idea, but it's no longer urgent that we believe it. The pain has become too familiar.

But if our greatest hurts are really the wounds left by life-saving surgeries intended by God to bring about something truly wonderful, we don't have to clutch our pain so tightly. We don't have to settle for life with a limp. We can surrender our deepest hurts to Jesus and watch for ways he's working in our struggles to bring good things to us and glory to himself. This business of goodness and glory can take on many forms, the fullness of which may not be fully realized for many years. But that doesn't mean we should discount God's promise to use every broken dream and every tear-stained regret in this way.

The World Made New

One of the peculiar things about Christians is that we believe in resurrection. Against what our experience teaches and what the laws of nature would command, we who know Jesus believe that life can come from death—someone who was once alive and is now dead can be made new again. We believe in Jesus' resurrection from the dead two thousand years ago. We believe the biblical accounts of people like Lazarus being called back from death to life, and we look forward to the resurrection of believers at the end of the age. In fact, resurrection is the hope of the Christian life. Without it we are, as Paul wrote, "of all people most to be pitied" (1 Corinthians 15:19).

Our good God is in the business of breathing

new life into dead things. But we who are followers
of Christ also believe in another kind of resurrection. It's not just dead bodies that need new life. The
Bible tells us God is making all things new (Revelation
21:5)—even creation itself is looking forward to a time
when it will be set free from bondage and given new
life to the glory of God (Romans 8:19-21). New life is
the unswerving trajectory of redemption, and every
believer gets a taste of this resurrection-reality when we
are born again.

But here, in this world, we live in a blind spot. We
take *physical* to mean *real* and easily relegate that which
is *spiritual* to the realm of psychology and metaphor.
When we hear of "the new birth" we can think of
it as little more than a colorful description. But the
regeneration that phrase speaks of is nothing short of a
resurrection miracle—the Holy Spirit breathing new
life into a dead spirit. And because a spiritual resurrection is no less real than a physical one, the New
Testament speaks of this resurrection in the past tense:

> …You were also raised with him through faith…
> (Colossians 2:12).

> If then you have been raised with Christ…
> (Colossians 3:1).

> But God…even when we were dead in our tres-

passes, made us alive together with Christ…and raised us up with him (Ephesians 2:4-6).

As we come to know Christ and wake up to kingdom reality, we are resurrected. Little bits of future glory break into our dark world. Territory is taken for God's kingdom. Bonds are broken and healing takes place. It's an invasion of epic proportions.

Even the vilest of sinners imaginable—murderers, rapists, sex traffickers—experience a completely new spiritual life when they come to Christ. There is no limit to what God can do with a life yielded to him. There is no pre-conversion sin that can withstand the power of the resurrected Christ. There is no amount of spiritual brokenness that cannot be healed by the new birth. Sin certainly has consequences, and people often have to live with those consequences long after coming to know Jesus. But those consequences are limited at the very most to this life, and they do not bind God's resurrection power in any way.

Why then do we balk at this same power when we experience severe heartache? When my marriage ended I didn't doubt God's love for me, but I believed my life was ruined beyond hope of repair. Any future I could have would be a "making do"—a consolation prize. I came to understand that believing this way is the opposite of faith, and an insult to our heavenly Father. We are like Ezekiel in the valley of dry bones, when he was asked, "Son of man, can these bones live?" And no matter what mountainous pile of death we're standing in the middle of, we have no right to any answer other than, "O Lord GOD, you know" (Ezekiel 37:3). Our God is good—so, so good—and he is in the business of bringing life to places where only death remains.

The Shape of Every Good Blessing

But there is a danger in this line of thinking. If we're not careful, we can begin to place our faith in some future *set of circumstances*. For someone like me who's walked through the pain of abandonment and divorce, it is natural to hold out hope for a new relationship, possibly a new marriage and family. For other pains, there are other hopes, but the danger is the same: we'll seek the gifts, rather than the giver. Something other than Jesus may become the object of our faith. This is nothing short of idolatry.

There is another danger too—an equal but opposite one. When we stop trusting God for good things, we can begin to imagine we're on our own. We can push Jesus so far out of our everyday lives that we no longer trust in his goodness or power—at least not in any practical sense. This is a way of minimizing risk, of lowering expectations, of not getting our hopes up too high. But this is really just idolatry in another form. When we stop looking to Jesus as our hope and the source of all good things, we invariably place our hope in someone or something else—our own perseverance, an important relationship, a certain pleasure, or one of a million other false gods.

There have been seasons in my own life when I've slipped—oh, I'll just admit it—when I've lunged right into idolatry. I've placed my hope in and allowed my joy to hinge on my circumstances. I've sought Jesus the way he was sought by the five thousand, looking only for the shallow blessing of miracle-bread, instead of the immeasurable pleasure that comes from knowing the bread of life. At other times, I've stopped hoping God could make something out of the mess of my life. I've settled for my lot and frantically taken control of the wheel.

The problem with these approaches (other than the fact that they're transgressions against the King of the universe, of course) is that they are hopelessly reckless. They don't take reality into account. They imagine that some perfect set of circumstances will satisfy our souls. But the truth is, nothing will ever satisfy us—nothing but Jesus. So when we seek to find our hope and joy in what seems like a best-case scenario or a unique set of blessings, we are setting ourselves up for disappointment. And when we try to minimize our disappointment by taking control of our lives and pushing Jesus out of the driver's seat, we will simply compound our disappointment. Jesus is the only satisfaction and rest our souls will ever find.

So then is it unholy—sacrilegious—to want God's blessings here and now, to desire anything at all other than him? In the valley of pain I walked through following the divorce, I wavered back and forth. Some days I would resolve to know nothing but Jesus, sensing that a self-imposed monasticism would be the only God-honoring choice to make with my life. Other days I would feel guilty for wanting to be married again. But as hard as I tried I couldn't deny my heart's desire for love, for a family, and for all the blessings that would come with marriage. And because the end of marriage cost me my job as a pastor, I also longed to walk in my calling once again—to teach the Bible, to spend my days invested in a local church, and to help people come to know Jesus in a deeper way.

I came to see that my heart's cravings were not sinful in and of themselves. In fact, inasmuch as those desires were good and beautiful, they could be traced back to God. He is the author of all good things, and by his redemptive power, all of history will culminate in a heaven-meets-earth kingdom where the good, true, and beautiful will burst forth from every molecule in new creation, no longer tainted by sin, death, and heartache. The problem comes when I let my desire for the good overshadow my desire for Jesus.

The answer is not to deny those desires, but to give them over to Jesus, no matter how much it hurts to let them go. When we give our dreams over to him, we don't stop dreaming. Rather we refocus our hope away from the particular gift and fix it on the giver. This is the only way to keep otherwise good desires from becoming idols which stand between Jesus and us.

As I thought about what this sort of yielded longing looks like, a few biblical examples came to my mind. I thought of Shadrach, Meshach, and Abednego standing before King Nebuchadnezzar and his furnace, and how they put their hope in God rather than mere rescue from impending death. I thought about Stephen, who was stoned to death for his faith in Jesus—how he never saw safety as the point of it all, but instead found contentment in the love of his Savior. But then I remembered the most powerful example of all—that of Jesus himself.

Alone in prayer in the Garden of Gethsemane, Jesus knows his own crucifixion is imminent. But more terrible than death on a cross, he knows he is going to be *made sin*. The wrath of God for the sins of the world is going to be poured out upon him. And he asks his Father to change his circumstances. "Father, if you are willing, remove this cup from me" (Luke 22:42).

Jesus, the very Son of God, the second Person of the Trinity, had a heart-desire to see his situation change. This part we can all understand. At one time or another every one of us—whether we've walked through the pain of divorce or not—has wanted life to be "fixed" in some way. It's what Jesus prayed next that is difficult: "Nevertheless, not my will, but yours, be done" (Luke 22:42). This is what it sounds like when a hope is yielded to God—when the greatest desire of a heart is to know God above all else.

When this is the order of our priorities, we are freed from bondage to our circumstances. Like Jesus, like Stephen, and like Shadrach, Meshach, and Abednego, we can respond to an uncertain future with unwavering resolve—regardless of our current struggles or what the future may hold. And we can be content without denying the reality that things aren't where we might like them to be. We can say with the Psalmist: "The LORD is on my side; I will not fear. What can man do to me?" (Psalm 118:6)

Fighting in the Sovereign Goodness of God

I know how it can sound. We live in a culture that champions the fighter, the overcomer, and the self-made man. All this talk of yielding our desires to God and looking to him alone smacks of giving up—of floating along, taking each wave as they come, rather than violently swimming against the current. It seems weak—the option of last resort when every other effort has failed. This is probably why my own spirit struggled with giving my pain and desires over to Jesus. It felt like I was conceding defeat to every one of my fears. But that was before I discovered that true strength lies in surrender to the Lord.

David understood this when no one else did. The men of Israel are lined up on one side of the Valley of Elah. On the other side stands the army of the Philistines, poised for battle behind their champion Goliath of Gath, who taunts Israel and her God. It's a familiar tale. David shows up during one of these taunting sessions and commits to fight Goliath, though he is woefully small in comparison. And with a sling and five stones (though he only needs one), David topples the oversized Philistine, and then cuts off his head in victory.

We call it a "David vs. Goliath" battle when an underdog takes on a much bigger opponent and wins. We marvel at people with "David's" skill—their strength, their strategy, or their smarts. But the ultimate reason David won that day was because he fought as a man wholly submitted to God. The victory was the Lord's, first and last, for David contributed nothing that God had not sovereignly worked in him. God could have used anyone he had chosen to prepare for that battle. In fact, God's choice of David—in all his welterweight youthfulness over against the massive Goliath—was a statement of God's power.

At the same time, however, David *fought*. The submission of his will to God's was *active*. He volunteered for battle. He convinced Saul to put Israel's fate on the line and let him fight. He gathered the stones. He stood his ground. And when the time came, he sunk a stone into the forehead of an enemy every other man in Israel was afraid to face. To paraphrase St. Augustine, David trusted as if everything depended on God, but worked as though everything depended on him.

This is what it looks like to live in yielded submission to God and to seek his glory above all else. It takes fighting, striving, seeking, and working. It means stepping out in faith and taking risks. David had no guarantee he would be successful, but he knew who God was and that God had promised Israel victory over her enemies.

We are not Israel. God has not declared temporal victory over every obstacle we face so long as we trust him. We may face disappointment after disappointment. We may try, we may fight, and we may give it everything we've got. And we may lose. Big time. But we serve the same God David did. And that God can still be trusted. He is sovereign, ruling over every tear-filled circumstance and hardship. And he is good, not allowing anything into our lives without purpose. If he has allowed it in, it has meaning. There is good that will be birthed from it, no matter how sharp our pain. We have no guarantees in our aches and struggles beyond this. And it is enough.

Three
WHAT SHALL I ANSWER YOU?

About three months after my marriage ended, I had one of those days that made me feel like my life might finally be taking a turn for the better. I was at a farmer's market with my sister, trying to embrace my new life in Georgia. I happened to be wearing a T-shirt from my alma mater, Gordon College, and had just passed a booth of homemade pies when a man selling honey tapped me on the shoulder and asked, "Excuse me, son. Did you go to Gordon?"

Gordon College is a very small Christian liberal arts college, just north of Boston. I was shocked that the honey man had heard of it. Not many people this far south had. "Yes, I did," I replied. And we began talking. He was a Yankee, too—a retired pastor from New Jersey. He was familiar with Gordon College and with Gordon-Conwell Theological Seminary, where I had done my master's work; he had sent students from his church to both schools. As it turned out, we had much in common. In fact we had once lived just a few miles apart in Connecticut and even had a few mutual acquaintances.

After a while, the honey man asked me what I did for a living. I explained I was a pastor but was still looking for work in Georgia. He smiled, and then he invited me to visit his church the next Sunday. There was someone he wanted me to meet.

I walked out of the farmer's market encouraged and excited. After months of feeling that my life was at a dead-end, God seemed to be answering my prayers — finally. I didn't know a soul in Georgia outside of my family, but the honey man had a job lead for me. Incredible.

Disapproval Wrapped in a Bow

The next Sunday I headed out to church. I arrived a little early and made my way to the sanctuary. I kept one eye on the door, waiting for the honey man to arrive, but soon the service started, and there was still no honey man. I was worried that perhaps he had forgotten about me. Maybe something had come up, and he had to miss church. Maybe God really wasn't answering my prayers after all. When the pastor finished his sermon, he asked the congregation to stand for the benediction. I looked around the room — maybe I had missed him when he came in. But there was no sign of him.

I walked out of the sanctuary disappointed. I don't normally get excited about networking opportunities, but at this low point in my life I was looking forward to meeting someone who might be able to help me find a job, especially if it was a job in ministry. As I headed for the door I heard a voice from the other side of the lobby. "There you are!" It was the honey man walking straight toward me with a smile on his face and an outstretched hand. He gave me a strong handshake, and then he grabbed me by the shoulders and said, "Wait right here. There's someone I think you should meet." And he disappeared into the crowd once more. When he returned he had in tow an older gentleman wearing a blue sport coat and a yellow bowtie. The honey man made the introductions, and then he stepped away. The older man was one of the founders of a major evangelical denomination in the United States and would make a powerful ally in my job search.

I liked the bowtie man immediately. He was kind, charming, and as it turned out, he knew just about everyone. We talked for about twenty minutes. He asked me about my ministry experience, my theological convictions, and about what sort of position I would like to find. And then he asked me, "Are you married?" I said, "Yes," and then paused for a moment before finishing. "The divorce is not yet final." The color left the bowtie man's cheeks, and he backed up a step or so. "Well, then," he said, "The best you can hope for is to work at a Waffle House. Good luck to you." Then with a handshake and a half-smile, the bowtie man turned and left without another word.

For weeks thereafter I replayed the meeting with the bowtie man over and over in my mind. *Waffle House? Seriously? That's all he thinks I can do with the rest of my life?* I hadn't done anything to disqualify myself from ministry—I didn't commit adultery, I didn't neglect my wife, and I fought for my marriage—but now, it seemed I was reaping what someone else had sown.

There is, of course, nothing wrong with working at a Waffle House, or at any other restaurant. In fact, it's good, honest work. Not only am I personally thankful for purveyors of midnight-breakfast goodness like Waffle House, but I also believe that if we do a job as if we're reporting directly to God, it brings him glory and honor (Colossians 3:23-24), regardless of the uniform, the pay, or the proximity to bacon. My dismay at the bowtie man's comment had to do with the dismissive and judgmental attitude he had toward me at the mention of the word *divorce*. Without knowing the first thing about my story, my marriage, or my heart, the bowtie man considered me unfit for ministry or any other work, save what he considered to be menial.

There is a part of me that would like to use the rest of this chapter to tell you how the bowtie man got his comeuppance—how I proved him wrong and got the best of him. But the truth is I haven't seen the bowtie man since that initial encounter. There is a part of me that would relish getting the best of him—that would love to see him eat his judgmental words—but that part of me grows deep in the soil of self-righteousness. And self-righteousness is a far more dangerous enemy than a disparaging old man with a bowtie.

Messy and Muddy

The bowtie man's response hurt, but it wasn't the only time someone has winced after hearing a bit of my story. In the last couple of years it's happened more times than I'd like to remember. When the subject of my marriage and divorce comes up, I brace myself. Though some people are kind and understanding, I'm never quite sure what to expect. Divorce is a big subject, and it seems everyone has an opinion and his or her own way of navigating the issue.

There are few who would deny that divorce is painful for everyone involved. Both spouses must deal with tremendous heartache, and they often carry baggage for years to come. They are commonly met with significant financial and relational challenges. Children of divorce face an uphill battle socially, economically, and even spiritually. Divorce also affects the couple's friends, family, church, and community. Like a wave on the ocean, the ripples extend far beyond the initial swell. No one benefits from divorce (except maybe the lawyers). No one wins. On top of that, God's Word tells us that he designed marriage to be a lifelong commitment (Genesis 2:24). It's not supposed to end; it's just not right or natural (see Malachi 2:16). No matter how you slice it, divorce is bad. Period.

Still, most Christians grant that Jesus permitted divorce on the grounds of adultery or other sexual sin (Matthew 5:32). In addition, Paul taught that divorce in the case of abandonment by an unbelieving spouse is also acceptable (1 Corinthians 7:15). Divorce may be a bad thing, but it is permissible—even for a believer— under certain conditions.

Although divorce is always the result of sin, both parties are rarely equally at fault. We rationalize that it takes two to tango, so both spouses must be to blame—at least to some extent. We imagine that for a marriage to end, both people must turn their keys at the same time, like firing torpedoes from a submarine. But divorce is rarely a mutual decision. This makes divorce messy and muddy. It doesn't fit neatly into our categories of "sin" or "not sin." Certainly, filing for divorce can be a sin, but not always. Each case is different, so it will not do to lump every divorce into one category or the other. But it would be easier, wouldn't it?

About a year after my divorce I was seated in the back of a church, listening to a pastor speak about relationship-oriented evangelism. In describing love he tossed out this one line: "Divorce is what happens when there's no unconditional love," and then he moved on. This wasn't a sermon about divorce or even about marriage—it was about evangelism. Yet there was this one, quick, out-of-place warning about divorce. And it stung. No qualifications. No exceptions. No nuances. With what I've been through, this one sentence lingered in my head (though I doubt it stuck in the minds of those around me in the same way). I felt attacked, accused, and condemned. I had loved my former wife without condition and I had remained faithful to her, but in the back of that church, it felt as if a guilty verdict had been rendered against me, and by someone who hadn't even met me.

I freely admit I'm extra sensitive to any mention of divorce from a pulpit. I wish this pastor had been more careful in his choice of illustrations that morning, but I don't think he meant any harm. In fact I think his heart's intentions were good. Marriage is tough, and it needs to be fought for. Husbands and wives need all the encouragement, counseling, prodding, and godly admonition they can get in order to fight the good fight. A pastor who's soft on divorce might appear soft on marriage too, and that would be dangerous. Divorce is regularly preached against in conservative churches, as it should be. Warnings are issued. Cautionary tales are told. Blanket statements are made. Suddenly, the messiness and muddiness of divorce disappear, and it becomes a black-and-white issue. In the minds of many people, divorce gets tossed into the "sin" category, along with adultery, murder, and theft. And both parties in a divorce are seen as being at fault—every time. It's just simpler that way.

This oversimplification of a complicated issue like divorce is all too common. It's human nature to classify, organize, and move on. We want to know where to stand and then rest. It's uncomfortable to have tension, and we like to have neat lines drawn. Lines make it easier to avoid ending up on the outside, away from our tribe, our team, our family.

Christians are not unique in this, and it's not only the subject of divorce where hard lines are used to this effect. It's part of the human experience, part of living in a sinful world. Just ask a single mother on food stamps what it's like to hear about the need to rein in welfare so people like her will stop mooching off of the system. Talk to the young man struggling with homosexual feelings but trying to follow Christ, who has listened to Christian leader after Christian leader teach that homosexual tendencies, and not just the behavior, are a choice. Seek out a pastor labeled a sellout and a compromiser because he freely tosses out cultural expressions of the faith in an imperfect but passionate attempt to reach the lost.

I am convinced that most Christians have at one time or another been burned because they have wandered outside of the camp and across the lines.

Even in writing this, I realize I run the risk of appearing soft on sin and morality. Some will read this chapter and conclude that I don't believe there are lines that can be crossed at all or that I believe all truth is relative. (For the record, I do believe in absolute truth, that sin is real and has consequences, and that there are indeed lines not to be crossed.) This very danger illustrates the point I'm trying to make: in our desire to understand and organize complex issues, we sum things up simply and neatly—but too often we clean things up the way a tsunami washes a beach clean, destroying people in our wake.

Drawing Our Own Lines

The funny thing about drawing lines is that it works both ways. Men and women familiar with the sting of being categorized, classified, and put into a box are not immune from the doing the very same thing to other people. The result is that we put ourselves on a seat of judgment—even to the point where we may determine God is acting unjustly in our struggles.

Job experienced this. He was a man described as "blameless and upright, one who feared God and turned away from evil" (Job 1:1). God himself said there was "none like him on the earth" (Job 1:8), but his friends saw how he suffered the loss of his family, his livelihood, and his health and concluded that his sin was to blame. It wasn't, of course. We, as the readers of

Job's story, get a glimpse behind the curtain separating heaven from earth. We see that God has allowed Job's physical pain, financial loss, and personal heartache in order to bring himself glory. Job's struggles are not the direct result of his personal sin, yet he suffers incredibly.

His friends surmise that Job *must* have done something terrible—even worse, he refuses to repent and receive God's forgiveness. They have taken the complicated issue of human suffering and made it neat, tidy, and easy to understand. Their thinking goes like this: God is good, therefore, good people won't suffer. In God's righteousness he will punish unjust sinners. So they reason that since Job is suffering tremendously, he cannot be innocent. He must have sinned against God to deserve what has come upon him.

Again and again Job answers his friends. He declares his innocence and his faith in God Almighty, but his friends remain undeterred. Nothing Job says will make them abandon their neatly drawn lines and useful boxes.

Job becomes frustrated, not only with his friends who refuse to listen to his defense, but with God too. "God has cast me into the mire, and I have become like dust and ashes. I cry to you for help and you do not answer me; I stand, and you only look at me. You have turned cruel to me; with the might of your hand you persecute me" (Job 30:19-21).

Job is crying out to God for help—to be justified

before his friends and neighbors—but God does not answer. The fervor with which Job appeals to God turns into accusation. Having already said that Job himself answers the call of the poor and the helpless (Job 29:12), he accuses God of not doing likewise—of being less than completely righteous. He has taken something he doesn't fully understand—his own suffering—and drawn his own lines. And this time it is God who is on the outside.

"I am righteous. I am innocent. I don't deserve this!" we cry out. We go to God with our case, asking him to set things right, to make others see the light, and to ease our pain. But seldom does God answer right then and there, fixing things precisely as we hope he will. Often his answer is simply, "Don't be afraid. I'll walk through this with you." God is sovereign over everything in the universe, so we can know that every painful situation we face has been sanctioned by our good God before ever coming into our lives. This means our struggles are never due to a divine mistake or the result of God looking the other way for a moment. God has ordained that we walk through what he has given us.

God's purposes are greater than ours, and he sees what we cannot. During times of frustration and heartache, it can be difficult to make sense of what God is working through us and around us. After repeated pleading sessions with Jesus, we can fall into the same trap as Job, believing that God owes us something. We draw this conclusion without all the facts, supposing we know more about the way things should be than God himself. In our hearts and our minds, we declare our own innocence at the expense of God's own righteousness.

But God does not owe us an explanation. God is not accountable to us. That is, of course, not to suggest that God betrays his own righteousness when it suits him. God is love, and he is holy, holy, holy. He carries with him not even a speck of corruption. He is good and trustworthy, but he doesn't need to tell us why he allows certain things to happen. He didn't need to tell Job the reasons for his suffering, and he doesn't need to give us an explanation either. I suspect if you or I were to hear audibly from God, our complaints would receive the same response as Job's: "Where were you when I laid the foundation of the earth? Tell me, if you have understanding. Who determined its measurements—surely you know! Or who stretched the line upon it?" (Job 38:4-5). God answered Job's questions with more questions, all of which pointed to one undeniable fact: *He is God and we are not!*

If we are wise, we will say to God, in both the stillness and the storms of our hearts, as Job did, "Behold, I am of small account; what shall I answer you? I lay my hand on my mouth. I have spoken once, and I will not answer; twice, but I will proceed no further" (Job 40:4-5). In other words, "You are God. I am not. I will shut up now."

The Guilt of the Innocent

When our lives seem full of bowtie men and others who will trample us, tear us down, and toss us aside, we turn to God for vindication and justice, not unlike Job. Even when we recognize that God is good, and that in his perfect, incomprehensible wisdom, he has allowed and directed the very stony path of pain we're traveling, we are in danger of falling into another kind of trap.

When my divorce was finalized, I took comfort in the fact that it wasn't my fault. I wasn't glad to have gone through the pain, but I could hold my head up, knowing I was the innocent one—the good guy. I had kept my marriage vows and acted with integrity. Was I perfect? Of course not, but my conscience was clean. The more I encountered people like the bowtie man, the more I took solace in my innocence. But as I discovered, there's a thin line between innocence and victimhood.

I mentioned earlier that both parties rarely share equal blame for a divorce. This is true. Marriage is, by definition, two sinners doing life together. To be sure, both a husband and wife will bring recurrent sin issues, selfishness, and their own brand of brokenness into a marriage. But in most cases of divorce (though certainly not all), one person acts unilaterally to break the covenant and shatter the marriage.

In my own situation, my former wife had an affair, deciding beforehand that she did not want to attempt reconciliation. No doubt I sinned against my former wife repeatedly in our seven and a half years of marriage. Though I did my best to love her like Jesus, I'm sure there were a number of ways I failed her as a husband. Even so, there's a big difference between committing adultery and hogging the TV remote. All sins in a marriage are not equal!

When the dust settles after a marriage breaks in two, one half of the former couple will often shoulder a great deal of guilt and shame. Knowing you have sinned against God and your spouse is a heavy burden. The other half of the former couple may experience a measure of guilt as well, knowing that, despite one's best efforts, it seemed impossible to keep the marriage together. This person can also feel victimized — innocent, but suffering unjustly for the actions of the ex. Left unchecked, these feelings can turn deadly serious — bitterness, pride, and idolatry spread like bacteria in these waters. Both people need healing. Both people need Jesus.

One party bears the lion's share of guilt, the other suffers as a victim, but both need forgiveness. This may be tough to understand, but it's a situation as old as the Israelite exodus from Egypt. In the story, there's a clear "bad guy" and a clear "good guy." The Egyptians are the bad guys, keeping God's people in bondage and denying the power of the one, true God. The Israelites are the good guys, crying out to the God of their ancestors in faith and trusting he will rescue them from their yoke of slavery. We would expect that God would come and smite the Egyptians and save the Israelites. But actually, God comes ready to smite everyone—everyone who isn't sealed with Passover blood (Exodus 12:12-13). When the Lord arrives, ready to take care of the bad guys, he makes no distinction between Egyptian homes and Israelite homes. He only passes over those houses covered with the blood of a lamb, leaving the firstborn in the blood-homes to see the morning. Both the good guys and the bad guys stand ready to be judged. It is only those who come to Christ—the Lamb to whom the Passover lambs pointed—who will find forgiveness and rescue.

When we know we're guilty, our consciences and the Holy Spirit drive us to seek forgiveness and rescue, but when we've been victimized, it's not always so obvious. In Luke 15, Jesus tells the parable of the Prodigal Son. The story ends with a party, but do you remember who misses out—who remains outside while the fatted-calf-kabobs are passed around and the music is playing? "But [the older brother] was angry and refused to go in" (Luke 15:28). In the parable, the older brother was the "good" one, the obedient one—the innocent one—who hadn't wished his father dead or squandered his inheritance. But his younger brother—the ungrateful, selfish, lazy, reckless, prostitute-visiting lush—felt the weight of his sin and returned home. Though he didn't deserve it, he received healing and restoration. At the end of the story, it's the younger brother who's enjoying the love of his father, something the older brother simply refuses to do.

The younger brother had no one but himself to blame for his actions. He nearly lost everything through his self-centered, arrogant, and lustful choices. But because his sin had very painful consequences, he recognized his brokenness and his need for healing. And he found it. His father's welcome was like a pardon given to him on death row—a new lease on life and an unspeakable mercy completely undeserved.

The older brother, on the other hand, had been a victim of his brother's selfish escapades. Remember how the younger brother had demanded his share of the inheritance from their father? In those days property was wealth, so in all likelihood the father had to sell off some of the family's land in order to give his younger son his inheritance early. But that's not all. After the prodigal returned, his father restored his position as a son, with all the rights and privileges a son could expect. He was back in the will once again. The older son—through no fault of his own—would now receive a smaller inheritance.

While the older son was just as broken as his younger brother, his brokenness was of a different sort. He had tried to earn his father's blessing through obedience and hard work. He didn't see the need for restoration, for healing. He didn't see that he was broken at all—that he, too, needed unspeakable mercy. As a result, when an invitation to the party was extended to him, he refused to take part. He refused to live in his father's love. Victims do this because they only see the sins committed against them. Sadly, they often pass up the very love they need in order to heal.

The Bible declares, "None is righteous, no, not one" (Romans 3:10). And if we understood the depth and magnitude of our sin, we would be compelled to acknowledge that no part of our life has been left untainted. The prophet Isaiah says even our good deeds are like "filthy rags" before the Lord (Isaiah 64:6, NIV). The effort I took to love my wife like Jesus? Filthy rags. The way I honored my marriage vows? Filthy rags. My decision to be kind and not vengeful through the divorce process? Filthy, stinking rags. There is nothing I can stand on to declare my innocence. The truth is I need forgiveness and healing just as much as my former wife. And so do you—no matter what your story is. Jesus stands ready to forgive, to heal, and to restore, but all too often we crumple up the pardon notice and toss it aside, perhaps a little insulted, believing we have no need of forgiveness.

Each one of us carries baggage from living in a sinful, fallen world. We've all been hurt, and we've all hurt others. We need the forgiveness and the restoration that only comes when we surrender our burdens to Jesus. If you've walked through the heart-wrenching pain of divorce, you may carry the weight of knowing that your actions caused the end of your marriage, or you may see yourself as the one who was sinned against, victimized, and left on the side of the road. Either way, Jesus is the only place to go with your guilt, your shame, your burdens, your baggage, and your heart's biggest questions. Every last one of us is broken, and no amount of crushing guilt or deep-wound bitterness disqualifies us from turning to the only one who can give us relief and make us whole.

When all of this sank in, I made a conscious decision to pay no mind to the voices of friends and family telling me how despicably my former wife had acted. While their intentions may have been good— trying to alleviate any guilt I might have had over my inability to keep the marriage together, while at the same time assuring me I would be better off without my former wife—my heart took those statements and bent them inward so that they fueled a latent desire to get even and provided me with an unwarranted license to live selfishly. Those statements would fool me into believing I was a victim and that my victimhood earned me a right to indulge in certain prideful, self-centered sins without consequence. Even though this particular path is often traveled slowly, it's one that steadily leads a person away from God. God was the one thing I needed and the source of every good thing in my life. I knew I would find no greater joy than him, but that didn't mean that following his will for my life in the aftermath of my divorce would be easy. In calling us his children, he calls us to live up to the family name.

Four
CHRIST, OUR EXAMPLE

When my former wife decided to commit adultery and walk away from our marriage, she hurt me deeply—more deeply than anyone before or since. She cost me financially; I lost money, shared possessions, and even a job. She cost me relationally; I lost friends and family on her side of things. And she cost me emotionally; there were plenty of sleepless nights and tear-filled days. She even cost me a bit of my hair! (It started to fall out from stress in the months following our split.) If ever there was someone to take off my list of people to love, it would be her. But Jesus says I can't.

Jesus says I must love my enemies. It's not a choice. Not a nice thing to do. Not an option. He commands it. Of all the bitter pills I faced following the crumbling of my marriage, this was the most difficult to swallow. But as it often is with medicine, the harsh taste led to healing.

Part of the difficulty with loving our enemies is

that love is both action and emotion. The action part is tough, but manageable. We all do things every day because we have to, not because we love doing them. It's the love-as-emotion part that's harder to muster. I knew God wanted me to be obedient, but more than that, he wants my obedience to flows from a heart in love with him! Anything else would be hypocritical. Anything else, and I would become the kind of person God lamented in Isaiah's time: "This people draw near with their mouth and honor me with their lips, while their hearts are far from me, and their fear of me is a commandment taught by men" (Isaiah 29:13).

Authentic Obedience

To borrow an illustration from John Piper, this kind of heartless obedience is like a husband coming home with a bouquet of flowers on his anniversary, mechanically handing them to his beautiful, faithful wife, and with a peck on the cheek, saying, "There. It's our anniversary. That's my duty. Enjoy."[3] Will she be happy? Of course not. She doesn't want the flowers; she wants her husband's heart. In the same way, God doesn't want my outward piety; he wants my love. Without a heart that longs for God, any outward act of love toward my former wife would be meaningless, dishonest, and dangerous. After all, it was the Pharisees—the people in his day who were the most outwardly obedient to God's law—for whom Jesus reserved his harshest criticism.

Authenticity—being *real*—holds a lot of weight in our world. We like people who seem genuine and honest. No one's perfect, so people who come forward with their shortcomings and moral failings may be preferred over people who try to hide who they really are. In one sense, this is good. We should cherish what is true and never live in denial or hypocrisy when it comes to sin. When Jesus puts religious hypocrites like the Pharisees in their place, I want to be standing in the front row and applauding. But sin must still be dealt with. You can't just "be real" about your sin and then move on as if all is well. Our culture's insistence on keeping things *real* is oftentimes a cartoonish overreaction that does nothing but celebrate our fallen world and give license to sin.

It's here the sound of my self-righteous applause fades away. Jesus' followers are called not to mere authenticity but to imitation. Hearts in love with Jesus will want to be like him even more than they want to be authentic. As we stumble along through life, our heart-obedience will always be imperfect. But the nature of the thing has changed. The Bible says that, as God's children, we have been given new hearts (see Luke 8:15, Acts 15:9, 1 Timothy 1:5, 2 Timothy 2:22). That which is truly authentic now for the Christ-follower is obedience, love, and the way of kingdom life. As Christians who have been hurt, trampled on, and left for dead, we are called to love people. And there are no exceptions. We are to love the very people who hurt us, trampled on us, and left us for dead—just as Jesus does.

Not for the Faint of Heart

Jesus knows a little something about being left for dead. He was tortured, mocked, spat upon, crucified, stabbed, and humiliated. Instigated by the religious leaders of his day, demanded by the crowds in Jerusalem, and sanctioned by the Roman government, Jesus was murdered. He endured the worst this world has to offer, and he did so without complaint—for you and for me and for the people who called for his death. He did so from a heart overflowing with love for the world and for God the Father. Having committed no crime, never lifting a finger to fight back, and cursing no one, Jesus gave up his life.

It wasn't only the Jewish crowds and the Romans who hurt Jesus. The Gospels record that when Jesus was arrested, his disciples scattered (Matthew 26:56, Mark 14:50). Judas, one from his inner circle of twelve disciples, betrayed him. Not one of the remaining eleven, with the exception of the beloved disciple (who was most likely John, the son of Zebedee; see John 19:26), stayed by his side during his time of immense suffering. His mother and a few other women were there, but his closest friends abandoned him, leaving him to die. It's difficult enough to deal with pain caused by strangers or our enemies, but the wounds of a friend hit harder, penetrate deeper, and last longer.

These words from the Psalms express a bit of what I felt when my marriage came crashing down around me: "For it is not an enemy who taunts me—then I could bear it…But it is you…my companion, my familiar friend. We used to take sweet counsel together; within God's house we walked in the throng" (Psalm 55:12-14).

It is not easy to forgive, let alone love someone who hurts us in this way. That's evident from the very next thing David writes: "Let death steal over them; let them go down to Sheol alive; for evil is in their dwelling place and in their heart" (Psalm 55:15). These words also express what I felt when I learned the truth about my former wife's betrayal. David's words of raw human emotion resonate with me. When someone hurts us, it's natural to have these strong feelings. Sin is an invader in our world—an alien, a parasite, and an infection. Our souls react when under fire.

Loving my former wife after she betrayed me was not easy. I walked the road of forgiveness, however imperfectly, not because she was lovable, but because Jesus is good. I discovered there are no simple formulas and no quick fixes. As I limped through the time of pain, I leaned on Jesus. I shared my heartaches and daily set my life's struggles and challenges at his feet. Looking back, what I learned about loving my former wife can be summed up in six movements. I believe these movements apply to loving anyone who's hurt us, and I believe these six love movements are exemplified in Christ's own life. None of them are easy, and none play nice with our old nature—the sin with which we wage war. These movements of love are not for the faint of heart.

Movement #1: Leave Vengeance with God

David's passionate plea for God to smite his friend-turned-enemy in Psalm 55 might seem to be the opposite of love. Requests like, "Let death steal over them" and, "Let them go down to Sheol [the grave] alive" are not quite the stuff of greeting cards. There can be no sugarcoating David's words to make them more palatable. He is asking God to kill the one who hurt him. But David's words are a far cry from vengeance. At face value, they seem fleshly and ungodly, but remember, God hates evil. At least in part, David's requests echo the heart of God.

One thing to note about David's prayer is that it contains a measure of restraint. He is leaving the fate of his enemies up to God. He asks God to handle them. He asks God to deal with their sin. David himself will not strike his enemies; that's God's prerogative and God's territory.

We see this lived out in David's story. King Saul wanted him dead, though David had done nothing to deserve his wrath, and twice he spared Saul's life (see 1

Samuel 24, 26). I don't think there's a jury in the world that would have convicted David, but he restrained himself, and God took care of Saul.

When I first heard the news about my former wife's affair, and when I first realized our marriage was over, I could not forgive. Not at first. But what I could do was give my desire for revenge—every part of me that wanted to make her pay—over to God. It took everything within me to take that simple step. I didn't wish her well. I didn't want her to get her life back on track. I certainly didn't want her to find forgiveness for what she had done. But until I *could* want those things, I could do as David did and put her fate in God's hands. I could ask God to deal with her, to do with her whatever seemed best to him. I yielded any thoughts of retribution to God. He is more just than I am. His ways are always higher than mine. We have no right to judge those who have trampled us and hurt us—but he does.

Romans 12:18-19 says, "If possible, so far as it depends on you, live peaceably with all. Beloved, never avenge yourselves, but leave it to the wrath of God, for it is written, 'Vengeance is mine, I will repay, says the Lord.'" This living at peace, this giving of vengeance over to God, can be seen throughout Jesus' trial, torture, and execution. At any moment, he could have called down legions of angels to destroy his tormenters (Matthew 26:53), but Jesus stayed his own hand. He let the madness continue, leaving it to God. "When he was reviled, he did not revile in return; when he suffered, he did not threaten, but continued entrusting himself to him who judges justly" (1 Peter 2:23). The night before in the Garden of Gethsemane, face to the ground, Jesus prayed, "My Father, if it be possible, let this cup pass from me; nevertheless, not as I will, but as you will" (Matthew 26:39). Of course, the *cup* Jesus spoke of was bigger than beatings, bigger than a crown of thorns, and even bigger than crucifixion; he knew he would bear the very wrath of God. But despite everything he was to face in the coming hours, he yielded himself fully to his Father.

Movement #2: Forgive

When I was still struggling through the deepest part of my grief, the thought of forgiving my former wife seemed heavy and cruel, another insult to add to the pile of hurt from which I was trying to dig out. It seemed almost a cliché—just too simple to say—I should forgive her after she sinned against me the way she had. Everything in me wanted to take forgiveness off the table, but every time I tried, I would stumble over Jesus' words: "For if you forgive others their trespasses, your heavenly Father will also forgive you, but if you do not forgive others their trespasses, neither will your Father forgive your trespasses" (Matthew 6:14-15).

Jesus wants us to forgive. But like everything God commands, it's for our own good. Forgiveness reflects what's in a person's heart, so an unwillingness to forgive suggests there is a weed of bitterness taking root. It turns out I needed to do some weeding. As a Christian forgiven by God, I had no right to withhold forgiveness from someone else. But forgiving would not come easily.

Forgiving my former wife, in my mind, would have been like pretending she had never committed adultery. I imagined it would be like telling her it was perfectly okay to treat me as she had. But that's not what forgiveness is. Forgiveness is never pretending your pain isn't real. It's never imagining the guilty to be innocent. Simply put, forgiveness is *letting go* of someone else's debt. It's a way of showing grace to another person, just as we have been shown grace by our Father. For there to be true forgiveness, there must be recognition and a reckoning of what's been lost. Forgiveness is never just letting offenses pass by like water under a bridge. When my former wife cheated on me, she cost me my marriage, my home, my job, family, friends, peace of mind—she rocked my world to its core. If I were to forgive her without stopping to examine what it is she'd taken from me, my gesture would have been insincere, fake.

So I examined, and I counted what was lost. I discovered that monumental, life-altering wrongs are rarely forgiven in one outing. I found that forgiving my former wife would take many moments of forgiveness over a long period of time.

As I went about the everyday business of living, I kept bumping into reminders of my losses, and each loss needed to be forgiven. One way this struck home was in my job search. Knowing my former wife's actions had already cost me a great job — my dream job in many ways — made the normal experiences of rejection and the need for patience in my job search that much more painful. With each new disappointment and with each person who looked at me disapprovingly, I had an opportunity either to hold on to bitterness or to release my former wife from her debt once more.

Forgiveness is a gift given from the injured to the injurer. It seems out of place in our always-get-even, look-out-for-number-one world. But in many ways forgiveness was more of a blessing to me, the forgiver, than it may ever be to my former wife. I could have internalized her choices as a statement about myself. I could have believed I had "lost my identity" since I was no longer a husband, no longer a pastor. And that's precisely what the enemy wanted. Satan longs for us to believe the lies that can be suggested to us by someone else's actions. But my identity is not to be found in being a husband or a pastor; it's only to be found in knowing Jesus, in being a child of God. By forgiving my former wife, I was stating emphatically that her sins against me, no matter how severe, had no power to write false words into my story. Only Jesus gets to write into my story, and his words are always true.

When Jesus had endured all the physical and emotional brutality this world had to offer, among his last words was a prayer of forgiveness for those who had tortured him, spat upon him, ridiculed him, and nailed him to a cross (Luke 23:34). Jesus was asking God to release them from their debt, to not hold these sins against them. He did this without a single person asking him for forgiveness.

My former wife has never asked me to forgive her, and I don't know if she ever will. Thank God that her repentance is not necessary for me to forgive her! Otherwise her sins against me would have the power to keep right on hurting me. I would have no choice but to hold on to her debts, and bitterness would continue to grow in my heart. Waiting for my former wife to come to me with an apology—carrying that grudge on my shoulders and in my heart—would be like drinking poison and hoping it harms her.

Movement #3: Pray

Jesus lived out his own words, "Love your enemies and pray for those who persecute you" (Matthew 5:44). In Jesus' prayer of forgiveness, "Father, forgive them, for they know not what they do" (Luke 23:34), Jesus was asking God, on behalf of his enemies, for what they needed the most—God's forgiveness. And as we see later in the New Testament, many of them repented and did indeed receive the forgiveness they so desperately needed (see Acts 3:17-4:4). Our prayers should seek what those who've hurt us need most—more of God. It's what we all need most.

As I thought about the sort of things that would truly bless my former wife, I asked God to make the call—to give her grace and bless her as he saw fit. Just as I had given any thought of vengeance over to God, I now yielded to him the job of blessing her. But as I prayed I could think of no greater blessing for a person to receive than more of Jesus, to be planted deep in the soil of the gospel.

Maybe she needed the Holy Spirit's conviction. We all need to have light flood those areas of life where sin still festers—places we may not even realize. Or maybe it's a desire for repentance that she needed. Every one of us needs to repent of the idols we hold up in the place of Jesus Christ. Or maybe what she needed most was the forgiveness of God. As we confess our sins to him, he promises forgiveness (1 John 1:9) and a closer walk with Jesus. He knows best, so I simply asked him to work in my former wife's life—to give her a life more joyful and God-honoring than any life she could fashion from her own efforts.

I struggled to spend my energy and time even thinking about my former wife who had caused me so much pain; praying for her often seemed impossible. But as I continued to do the work of forgiveness, prayer became a natural outflow—proof that the weeds of bitterness were being uprooted from my heart. At first, any prayer for her was difficult, but the more I did it, the more natural it became and the more God changed my heart so that I grew to want the best for my former wife.

Movement #4: Be Wronged to the Glory of God

Walking through pain is not about justice. We live in a broken world. In the present, some crimes will go unpunished, some debts will go unpaid, and some wrongs will go unanswered—at least for now.

Jesus told us to be prepared for injustice, to lean into it even. "But I say to you, Do not resist the one who is evil. But if anyone slaps you on the right cheek, turn to him the other also. And if anyone would sue you and take your tunic, let him have your cloak as well" (Matthew 5:39-40).

This way of living is contrary to everything our sinful nature screams for, but it's one of the ways that Jesus' followers declare the present and future kingdom. It's one of the ways we show that the old regime, with its eye-for-an-eye, tooth-for-a-tooth order, is passing away. It's one of the ways we act out our faith, showing that our hearts are wrapped up in Jesus and his kingdom, and not in this world. Love in response to hate is a bold statement. It's not easy; it costs something every time.

But love is not weak. It takes a lot more strength to stand under the weight of someone else's attacks without responding in kind than it does simply to pick up your sword and engage in the fight. It may seem the opposite—that the position of strength is the one that conquers by brute force, financial power, legal authority, or a sharp tongue—but it takes a lot more power simply to stand, turning your cheek as if to say, "Go ahead. Hit me again." When we take the position of love, we are wronged to the glory of God. King Jesus and his commands dictate our actions, rather than the instigations of our attackers. Soldiers in the army of the Lord are not weak—not in the slightest.

Matthew's Gospel tells us that when Jesus was on trial before the high priest, among the scribes and the elders, "They spit in his face and struck him. And some slapped him, saying, 'Prophesy to us, you Christ! Who is it that struck you?'" (Matthew 26:67-68). Jesus took their beatings and said nothing, but Jesus was not weak; he was not under any man's thumb. He was stronger than anyone who hit him or spat upon him. He suffered at the hands of the Jews and the Romans, not because they had greater power, but because he allowed them to hurt him, beat him, crucify him. Each drop of blood fell by his permission, his power. God had ordained the events of Jesus' suffering, and Jesus bore the weight of the cross for his own glory and for the Father's glory (John 17:1). The events of Good Friday were part of God's plan from ages past, and Jesus walked through them without complaint or grumble.

No one will gain eternal life because he suffers, but God has still ordained our struggles, our pain, and our trials. And more than that, he's ordained them for our good (Romans 8:28). Jesus' half-brother James wrote that we should be glad for them. "Count it all joy, my brothers, when you meet trials of various kinds, for you know that the testing of your faith produces steadfastness. And let steadfastness have its full effect, that you may be perfect and complete, lacking in nothing" (James 1:2-4).

James tells us that all the troubles that come our way are ordained by God to test our faith and bring about endurance, to make us more like Christ.

Every hurt in my life—every wound and every sorrow—first passed through God's loving hands. I can rest in the knowledge that, no matter how bad things may seem at times and no matter how much someone may hurt me, God is still in control. He has created this path for me to walk. I can either respond without faith, complaining and grumbling the whole time, or I can respond in hope, knowing that the dark colors I'm experiencing will one day become part of something beautiful God is painting. I can be wronged or I can be wronged to the glory of God.

Movement #5: Help the One Who's Hurt You

On the night Jesus was betrayed and arrested, he went peacefully, without fighting back. But there was one casualty. One of the servants of the high priest, a man named Malchus, lost his ear when Peter struck him with his sword. Peter was acting foolishly, thinking he was defending the Lord. He didn't yet understand that Jesus had to die and that Jesus was laying down his life; no one would *take it* from him. Malchus, for his part, was on the wrong side of history. He was among the mob there to arrest Jesus—to take him by force if need be. But Jesus loved his enemies and miraculously helped the man who came there to do him harm. "And he touched his ear and healed him" (Luke 22:51).

Just before my divorce was finalized, I received a call from my bank. Calls from the bank are never good news. Because my name was still on the auto loan for my former wife's car, they were contacting me to let me know they hadn't received her payment. In fact they hadn't received her last two payments, and the car was currently sitting in a police impound lot in California. The woman on the other end of the phone told me that, unless I made up for the late payments and fees, my credit report would be taking a massive hit in the next couple of days.

I was furious. It was just so wrong. My former wife had wanted the nicer, newer car, even though it was not yet paid for, and I generously agreed to let her have it. I took the car with the miles and the years and the dents and the broken air conditioner. My name was still on her car loan because the bank wouldn't let me remove it. She didn't have strong enough credit to get a loan of her own, so I was patiently waiting for her to get a full-time job, all the while fearing that something like this might happen. And now, she was going to drag my credit score through the mud because she couldn't keep up with the payments! And what was all this about the car being in police custody?

I got off the phone and went for a walk. And I prayed. At first I just vented, giving God all the reasons why this was just plain unfair. Then when I had gone through my list, I asked God what I should do. I waited and I listened. Listening is difficult when you're upset, so it took a while to calm my own heart enough to hear. I heard him say, not audibly, but as an impression on my heart: *Pay the debt.*

I didn't want to pay, so one more time I went through my list of all the reasons I shouldn't have to. But the more I thought about it, the more I knew it was the right thing to do. First, my name was still on the loan, no matter how much I didn't want it to be. My name was a pledge to pay, so when my former wife didn't, it became my responsibility. Second, even though our marriage was over, I was still legally her husband, for a few more days anyway. As such, it was my job to protect and provide for her. But more than all of that, I wanted to follow God, even if it meant taking another financial shot to the gut.

When I told people what I was doing, most said I was crazy. But I hoped that as I explained my reasons it brought glory to my Father in heaven. I know someday I will stand before God and answer for the way I handled my marriage—and my divorce. As he gives me opportunity, I want to be the kind of person who lives out the difficult commands of Jesus. "But love your enemies, and do good, and lend, expecting nothing in return, and your reward will be great, and you will be sons of the Most High, for he is kind to the ungrateful and the evil. Be merciful, even as your Father is merciful" (Luke 6:35-36).

Movement #6: Move Forward

Hebrews 12:2 tells us that Jesus, "for the joy that was set before him endured the cross, despising the shame." Jesus didn't get bogged down in the mire of the moment. His suffering was real—more real than any of us can know—but it wasn't where his heart was. He suffered on earth, but his focus was on heaven. He knew his mission, and he knew the Father was at work in what he had to do. So he pushed through. He endured. And he moved forward.

A season of pain can be like walking up the side of a mountain in the pouring rain with nothing on your feet but flip-flops. It's hard to survive, let alone move forward! Moving past all the pain and heartache sounds wonderful, but deep wounds have a way of lingering. When our world has been shaken, things may never go back to the way they were before, so any sense of normalcy seems elusive.

But you and I were not called to normalcy. We were not called to live clinging to the side of a mountain in our flip-flops. These seasons of pain will come— they are inevitable. But they will also go. Whether we're experiencing happiness or sorrow, our calling remains the same: to follow Jesus and bear fruit (see John 15:1-17). More than any other people on earth, we are truly called to have life to the full (John 10:10).

In the midst of a trial, we are invited to take every aching moment and every anxiety to the Lord. We can rest them on his shoulders, lean on him for daily strength, and seek him in everything we do. But God does not want us to linger in our pain any longer than necessary. We can walk through it for his glory, knowing it's only temporary. There is a time coming when everything will be made right, every tear will be wiped away, and mourning will be a thing of the past (Revelation 21:4). God is good, he can be trusted, and there is life beyond the darkness.

In the months following the end of my marriage, the path I traveled was a difficult one. It was certainly not a steady climb up out of the mire. There were dips and peaks, mountains and valleys, but as I reached out to Jesus day after day and week after week, I came to understand that the *normalcy* I was seeking had always been right there with me. One thing never changed, despite all the losses and all the heartache: Jesus was with me, just as he had been before. As the weeks and months rolled by, I learned that no matter where this path led me, Jesus would be there. It no longer mattered what happened next. Though I sometimes stumbled, I learned what Paul meant when he wrote, "I know how to be brought low, and I know how to abound. In any and every circumstance, I have learned the secret of facing plenty and hunger, abundance and need. I can do all things through him who strengthens me" (Philippians 4:12-13).

The secret Paul spoke of here is not really a secret at all. In fact, he tells us the secret: "him who strengthens." The secret is Jesus, the joy set before us.

Five
WAKING UP

"Do you really think this is how God wants us to see our marriage?" I asked my former wife. Sitting in a pastor's office, waiting for him to come back into the room, I thumbed through the book he insisted we read as a step in repairing our marriage. It was a popular book, published by a major Christian publisher. It was sprinkled with Scripture throughout and contained lots of personal testimonies about how effective the author had been in helping couples avoid divorce. But something about it didn't sit right with me.

"I don't know," she said, "but this is what he told us to read." This was several months prior to her affair, but my former wife had been hinting at divorce for some time. A few times she had dropped little statements in the air like, "Sometimes, I just think you'd be better off without me," or, "My life would be so much easier if I were single again." Each time, she had assured me she wasn't serious—that she was struggling to feel happy like she once did, but she remained committed to our marriage. Because I wanted to help her regain her joy and because I wanted a strong marriage, I asked her to go to counseling with me.

The pastor insisted upon using this particular book; it was the only one he used for marriage counseling. The last thing I wanted in our marriage counseling sessions was to seem argumentative and hard to work with, so I gave the book a shot. But about a chapter and a half in, I knew something was horribly wrong. When I finished the book, my suspicions were confirmed. According to this psychologist-turned-author, the premise of the book—the secret to a happy marriage— was to make a deal with your spouse. If your spouse will agree to do A and B to make you happy, you should agree to do X and Y to make your spouse happy. If she loves to go out to dinner, you should give up home-cooked meals, and if you like to have Saturdays for your golf game, she should resign herself to the single life one day a week. It was as simple as that. If both people give up something to make the other person happy, everybody wins.

At first this might sound like wisdom, a practical solution for dealing with conflicts in marriage. I think that's one of the reasons this book has gained such a following. Being able to compromise is an important skill to have in any meaningful relation- ship. A person who's never learned to compromise would make a horrible friend or roommate, let alone a spouse. More dangerous, though, is that this author tells people exactly what they want to hear: *You're unhappy because your spouse isn't fulfilling your needs like he or she is supposed to.* In other words, you have a natural right to be happy, and it's someone else's fault if you're not. One glaring problem with that view is that marriage isn't God's prescription for happiness, and it is never another person's job to make you content. Only Jesus can ever satisfy the deepest longings of a soul.

To Make Us More Like His Son

After a few more sessions with this pastor, we found another counselor—one who recognized that the only hope for a marriage in trouble is the power of the gospel. But as you know, my former wife chose not to heed his counsel. She abandoned our marriage and broke the covenant she had made with me and with God.

Ephesians 5, Paul's famous chapter on Christian marriage, does not describe a 50/50 split. There is no verse advising couples to make deals with each other to secure personal happiness. We do not read, "Wives, make your husbands happy, for this is your calling." Nor is there a note to husbands, "Remember to fulfill all her needs, or she'll be justified in walking out on you." Instead, Paul paints a picture of a husband and wife whose roles are defined by Christ. "Wives, submit to your own husbands, *as to the Lord*" (Ephesians 5:22). "Husbands, love your wives, *as Christ loved the church and gave himself up for her*" (Ephesians 5:25). And the point of it all? "This mystery is profound, and I am saying that it refers to Christ and the church" (Ephesians 5:32).

Paul does not bring up Jesus in his discussion of marriage merely as a good example to follow, nor is Christ-and-the-Church merely a good analogy for marriage. Paul says God's purpose in creating marriage, way back at the beginning of our story in the Garden of Eden (see Genesis 2:22-24), was that marriage between a man and a woman should be a picture of Christ and his Bride, the Church. Jesus loves the Church, he died for the Church, and he saved the Church. He did all this, "so that he might present the church to himself in splendor, without spot or wrinkle or any such thing, that she might be holy and without blemish" (Ephesians 5:27). Christ *is* holy and blameless; the Church is *becoming* holy and blameless. And as husbands imitate Christ and as wives imitate the redeemed Church, both become more like Jesus. This is God's purpose in marriage—to make us more like his Son.

Standing on the other side of divorce, I read passages like Ephesians 5 with a gaping sense of loss. Marriage is a gift—a means of becoming more like Christ—and a gift I no longer possessed. I began to wonder about the rest of my life. Maybe God would lead me to marry again, maybe not. But because marriage seems such an important part of the Christian life, I grew sad. Like many single people, I thought perhaps I was missing out on something special. Worse—having been married, I knew exactly what I was missing out on.

Some time ago, I came across my copy of the marriage book my former wife and I had been given in counseling. I threw it out—it's not something I would ever lend to anyone, nor would I read it again—but before I did, I thought once more about its message. I immediately felt convicted about my attitude. I realized that in this season of my life I had been believing the very lie the author had been peddling—that my joy depended on someone or something other than Jesus. Instead of looking to the gospel I was mourning my losses, stubbornly holding onto them in my heart until God replaced them with something else. Then a thought occurred to me, a thought I am ashamed to admit had taken me so long to have.

What if, just like in my marriage, God was using my divorce and its aftermath to make me more like his Son?

The Power of the Gospel

God's purposes are not thwarted just because my marriage ended, and they're not thwarted because of any other hardship, heartache, or hang-up we may walk through. The cross of Jesus Christ declares in no uncertain terms that God is for us. "He who did not spare his own Son but gave him up for us all, how will he not also with him graciously give us all things?" (Romans 8:32). God uses our strengths and our weakness, our circumstances and our relationships— everything in life—to make us more like Jesus; that's why he called us in the first place (see Romans 8:29-30, 1 Corinthians 15:49). When we believe that something— anything—in life could derail this purpose of God, we believe one of Satan's oldest lies: God is holding out on us (see Genesis 3:5).

In the months following the end of my marriage, it seemed like my life was just one loss after another, from tangible things like my home and my job to the intangible things like parts of my identity and my sense of security. Bit by bit, my life was stripped clean, to the point that I had trouble meeting new people— something essential when you're in a new place and need a new job. But I no longer knew what my life was all about. The simple conversation starter, "So tell me about yourself," filled me with dread. I had no response. *Who was I now? What was my life all about?* I really didn't know who I was anymore.

Many of the markers I had used to build my identity—my role as a husband, my job, my ministry, and even where I thought my life's story was headed— were gone. It felt like I had nothing left to cling to. At my weakest, I had a hard time believing God was using this time in my life for any good purpose. But God is patient. When I faltered, he lovingly picked me up and let me try again. And again. And again. In time, I came to learn that I wouldn't get back on my feet by my own effort, nor would it really help to put some artificial positive spin on things. Instead it was the gospel that would change everything.

Slowly but surely God spoke into my life through other people and through his Word, to remind me of my true and unchangeable identity in Christ. *Who I am because of the gospel* became the most precious thing in the world to me. Sadly, it took me losing almost everything to see this clearly, but I am thankful that God in his mercy took me to a place where I had nothing left to grasp but him. The foundations I had built for myself were faulty anyway, able to be shaken and blown apart by a stiff breeze.

Gospel reality, by contrast, is secure and immovable. God's love and care demonstrated at the cross remains true, no matter what comes our way. And it is often during the pressure of a severe trial that we come to know, in a way we simply couldn't before, that our identity in Jesus is the only thing that really matters. This identity disarms every insecurity and doubt because it loudly declares the truth about who God is and what he has done for us.

Redeemed Sinner: God is Able

John's Gospel records a scene in which Jesus heals
a man who was born blind (see John 9). Knowing
Jesus, it's what we expect him to do. What is a bit more
shocking is the question Jesus' disciples ask prior
to the healing event: "Rabbi, who sinned, this man
or his parents, that he was born blind?" (John 9:2).
Today, we tend to see diseases and handicaps as the
result of genetics and natural phenomena. Sin doesn't
really factor in. As believers we may argue all physical
ailments are the result of the Fall, that they're the
by-products of living in a sinful world, but we don't
attribute them to individual sins.

In Jesus' day, however, it was common to see a
disability like blindness as being directly caused by
a person's sin. Similar to the ethical theories of Job's
friends, it was believed a just God would never punish
someone unjustly with a physical impairment as
serious as blindness. In this particular instance since the
man had been blind since birth, the question was raised
whether this "punishment" of blindness was the result
of his own sin or caused by something his parents had
done.

Jesus of course sets the record straight. This man
was not born blind because of anyone's sin. We do not
live in a universe that runs on karma. Instead this man's
blindness was given so "that the works of God might
be displayed in him" (John 9:3).

I wonder what the blind man thought as he heard the conversation Jesus was having with his disciples. Did he believe his blindness was caused by his sin? Was every moment in darkness an apparent reminder that he was a failure, inadequate and broken? Was his opinion of God shaped by his handicap? Did he believe God was harsh and cruel? Or did he think God was merely weak, unable to forgive him and repair his sight? John's account gives us no insight into the man's state of mind prior to being healed. As far as we can tell from the text, Jesus rubs the healing spit-mud in the man's eyes before the man says a word to Jesus or his disciples.

At times I have felt what I imagine that blind man felt. Difficult burdens can appear to have all the markings of divine punishment for sin. Far too easily I turn God into a judge with scales in his hands, weighing my good deeds against my bad. Pain and heartache seem like a sure sign I am out of favor with God.

But this is faithless. This way of thinking nullifies the gospel in my life.

When I fail to trust in the completed work of Jesus, I believe a lie about God—that he is not powerful enough to remove my sin (completely!) and leave me pure, unspoiled, and clean (completely!). When things seem bleak and the world is crashing down all around us, this lie can seem plausible. You and I come face to face with our shortcomings and sins every day. It takes faith to know sin has been dealt with, once and forever on the cross.

It was there at the cross of Calvary that history's most imbalanced trade occurred — our sin for Christ's righteousness.

> This righteousness is given through faith in Jesus Christ to all who believe. There is no difference between Jew and Gentile, for all have sinned and fall short of the glory of God, and all are justified freely by his grace through the redemption that came by Christ Jesus (Romans 3:22-24, NIV).

It's scandalous, and that may be why it's so hard to believe, but God calls us *righteous* — you and me and anyone else who has come to know his Son, Jesus. We have been bought at a price. Under the shadow of the cross, we are no longer under the shadow of God's wrath. Instead we have been washed clean, made new, and reconciled to our creator.

The cross of Jesus loudly proclaims, "There is now no condemnation for those who are in Christ Jesus" (Romans 8:1). Any punishment my sin deserved was borne by Jesus on Good Friday. To be sure, sin still has consequences in this life, and God does discipline his children, but if we have been born again, we never have to wonder if God accepts us — the answer is a resounding *yes* in Christ. Knowing this gospel truth changes the nature of our struggles and our hardships. They are not arbitrary, and they are not the result of God's anger being poured out into our lives because we've missed the mark and disappointed him. They have meaning and purpose because, just like the man's blindness, they are circumstances through which the works of God might be displayed. Yes, we are sinners, but that's not the end of the story. Because of God's incredible power, we have been set free.

Vessel of the Holy Spirit: God Cares

One of the nicest parts of going through a divorce (if there can be such a thing) is the heartfelt emails and calls from friends and family offering genuine help. Right after I learned about my former wife's affair, a couple of friends came over to be with me. A few weeks later, one of those friends bought me a gas card to help with my cross-country drive. A few days after that, a pastor friend sent me some unexpected money. Then one of my former teachers sent me a check and a letter, telling me he knew God had some kingdom work for me to do in the future; he was happy to invest in it. My sister and her family opened up their home to me. Many, many people called to see how I was doing. And many, many more prayed for me. It was good to know I was loved and to know I was not alone.

God promises never to leave us or forsake us. But

God's definition of never leaving us goes much closer and much deeper than the people in our lives—even the most loyal of friends and family. God moves in. The creator and sustainer of the universe, the King of kings who carved out the oceans and who knows how many hairs are on your head, the commander of the angel armies who placed every star in the sky and who holds every moment of time in his hands, lives inside of you and me. Our bodies are his temple, the place where heaven and earth meet (1 Corinthians 6:19).

Before he was betrayed and turned over to the authorities to be crucified, Jesus promised his disciples: "I will not leave you as orphans; I will come to you. Yet a little while and the world will see me no more, but you will see me. Because I live, you also will live. In that day you will know that I am in my Father, and you in me, and I in you (John 14:18-20)."

Jesus would appear to his disciples after his resurrection, but here he is speaking of the coming Holy Spirit, *the Helper* whom God the Father would send in Jesus' name (John 14:26). When we come to know Christ, the Holy Spirit comes to live within us, not only to breathe new life into our dead spirits (Titus 3:5-6), but also to guide us into all truth (John 16:13), to empower us (Acts 1:8), to produce fruit in our lives (Galatians 5:22-23), to give us spiritual gifts (1 Corinthians 12:8-11, Hebrews 2:4), and to make us holy (2 Thessalonians 2:13, 1 Peter 1:2).

God comes to live within us because that has been his desire all along—to dwell with his people. Therefore we should never have any doubt God cares for us. The proof is that his Spirit lives inside of us. Still, when I found myself at the end of my rope, I questioned whether God was at all concerned with what I was going through. I wondered why he had allowed my life's path to take this rocky course. God knows these times will come in every one of our lives. The valleys may look different in the lives of different Christians, but doubts will always come when pressures increase and trouble surrounds. God gave us his Holy Spirit as a foretaste—a down payment—of what is to come, so when questions arise, we can have his assurance that he cares for us. He is "the guarantee of our inheritance until we acquire possession of it, to the praise of his glory" (Ephesians 1:14).

Ultimately the Holy Spirit's influence was a great comfort in my life. Oftentimes I could feel Jesus' presence and peace in a way words cannot express, a way that "surpasses all understanding," as Paul puts it in Philippians 4:7. When everything around me told me to panic, and when I had no earthly reason to hope, Jesus brought calm to my quaking heart. I can only explain these experiences by the Holy Spirit's influence and residence in my life. He is the unwavering affirmation to every heart that asks, *Does God really care?*

Child of the King: God Loves

C.S. Lewis wrote, "It is a serious thing to live in a society of possible Gods and Goddesses. To remember that the dullest, and most uninteresting person you can talk to may one day be a creature which, if you saw it now, you would be strongly tempted to worship."[4]

We are not what we once were, and though we have not yet been glorified as Lewis describes, the gospel has changed everything. Like being picked up off the street in the filthiest of ghetto slums and taken via private jet to live in a king's palace, we are adopted as God's children and made brothers and sisters of Jesus (Ephesians 1:5). At times this gospel promise seems just too good to be true. An understanding of the depth of our sin and disgrace must be overcome by a deeper knowledge of the magnitude of God's love and grace.

My former wife and I never had children. It's not that we didn't want a family; it just wasn't God's plan for us. Today I'm thankful we didn't have kids. I would hate to think of the pain they would have experienced because of our divorce. Perhaps it was God's grace that kept us from having a baby. Even as I talk about children that don't exist, I want to spare them pain—I want the absolute best for them. How much more does God, as our Father, creator, and sustainer, want the absolute best for us?

A gospel-centered life learns to recognize everything—even seemingly bad things—as being the very best from the hand of a loving God and Father. Jesus says,

Which of you, if your son asks for bread, will give him a stone? Or if he asks for a fish, will give him a snake? If you, then, though you are evil, know how to give good gifts to your children, how much more will your Father in heaven give good gifts to those who ask him! (Matthew 7:9-11, NIV).

The parallel passage in Luke 11:13 states that the good gift from the Father is the Holy Spirit. This is God's character. Just as earthly parents would never give their children stones or snakes to eat, neither will our heavenly Father. And though there are many times in life where it seems all we're receiving are pebbles and pythons, it only *seems* that way—everything, in one way or another, is given for our good. Big things like divorce, death, and disease, as well as smaller things like traffic, taxes, and termites, all have a purpose from heaven. We can know these purposes are good, because we who know Jesus are children of the King. He has made us his own, not to harm us or neglect us, but to love us.

The Beginning

Every Christmas, I have to watch *It's a Wonderful Life*. I know some people think it's over-the-top, saccharine sweet, but I love it. And every year it makes me tear up just a little bit. Of course I cover this up so no one else in the room can see my eyes water, but that movie gets me every time. There's something incredibly powerful about the final scene. Everyone in town, wealthy and poor, young and old, pulls together to help their friend, George Bailey. By this late moment in the film, you can see why: George Bailey has been a friend to each of them.

But that's not the way George saw his story. George believed his was a sad life, wasted and irredeemable. His dreams of leaving town and seeing the world, of making something of himself, had been thwarted time and time again. He never made a lot of money and wasn't able to give his family the life he had dreamed of.

Now, through no fault of his own, he faces a public scandal and prison time. He thinks the world would be a better place if he were dead, so he stands on the bridge leading out of Bedford Falls, ready to jump into the icy water and end his life. And when an angel is sent to help him, he takes it one step further, saying that he wishes he had never been born.

The angel, Clarence, then takes George on a journey through town, showing him what life would be like if he really hadn't been born. As it turns out, everyone is better off for knowing George; he has truly made the world a better place. All of this leads to a resurrection scene. George doesn't die physically, but he wakes up to new life. His eyes are opened to see he really has had a wonderful life. Every disappointment and discouragement, every lost dream and opportunity — they've all been used to make him into the man he's become and to help those around him. He finally sees the blessings in his life for what they are. Even when he still thinks he'll be going to jail, he is happy beyond measure, thankful for the life he's been given.

The final scene in the movie — the one that makes me shed a tear every time I see it — is not really the end of the story. It's only the beginning. From that point forward, George Bailey is no longer stuck in his circumstances, no longer a prisoner to what could have been — George Bailey gets to live the rest of his life knowing that life is good, no matter what the future holds.

When my marriage was over I felt like the life I had been building had collapsed, and all that was left was rubble around my feet. I never contemplated suicide like George Bailey, but I certainly felt like a failure, like my life was inconsequential to those around me and perhaps even to God. But God showed me that his plans for my life had not collapsed, that he would use even the hard places of divorce and unemployment for my good and for his glory. Today I can attest to that goodness as I reflect on my identity in Christ. Walking through these valleys has put flesh and bones on what it means to be a redeemed sinner, a vessel of the Holy Spirit, and a child of the living God. I have also seen God use the biggest disappointments in my life to

birth new beginnings I would have thought unimagi-
nable before—opportunities and joys I never would
have known without first experiencing the pain of my
marriage being broken to pieces.

Life is good. That's not to deny there are hard
patches, tough circumstances, and horrible losses. But
those things are the anomalies, the pieces that don't fit
the larger picture.

Life is good, because God is good.

Afterword
WHY I WROTE THIS BOOK

A few years ago, my then six-year-old nephew Joseph asked me why I was a writer. (He had heard me talking with his mother about a writing project I was working on.) At first, I took the easy way out. "Because I like to write," I said.

"Why do you like to write?" he asked.

"I like to write about the Bible and tell other people about Jesus," I said.

"But why do you like doing that?" Joseph pressed.

"Well, I think God made me to like it."

"Why?" he insisted.

And this went on for a few more rounds with him asking me "Why?" and me circling around the truth that I had no idea why I write much of anything. It's just something God has put in me. In the end, I distracted Joe with the promise of candy. But because I have no candy to offer you, and since I do know the Whys behind this book, I offer the following brief explanation.

For a long time, this book existed only as wishful thinking, or rather, whatever the opposite of wishful thinking is. I had the impression God might want me to write something about the path I trudged through the far side of divorce and its aftermath. But I didn't want to. I didn't want to spend any length of time wading back through painful memories, and I certainly didn't want to have my name in print next to the word "divorce." And so, the pages of this book remained locked away in my head, and I was happy to have them stay there.

But then I remembered those awkward conversations with people who have never been through something like what I've been through — the well-intentioned but uncomfortable (and sometimes hurtful) advice they offered, and the desperate loneliness and isolation I felt. In writing this book, my hope has been to bridge that gap, to stand alongside people who know the sting of divorce and other heartbreak, and at the same time, to inform those who've never known the pain personally. For many weeks and months following the end of my marriage, the hardest day of the week was Sunday. It's my hope that pastors, church leaders, and other Christians will find , after reading this short book, they have new and better words to say to the hurting.

Mostly, I wrote this book because I wanted to tell others about God's goodness. The gospel really does apply to every area of life. God really is making all things new. I have scars, but scars are reminders of where healing has taken place. And even these scars will not last forever.

A few days after I made the cross-country trek from California to Georgia, my nephew Joseph—the same little boy with all the Whys—had some more questions for me. He wanted to know about divorce. It was one of the saddest and hardest conversations I can remember. But when Joseph ran out of questions, he paused. Then he said something I'll never forget. With more sincerity and faith than should be possible for a boy his age, Joseph said, "Uncle John, it's okay. You're going to marry someone beautiful and have lots of kids."

As I type out these pages, I'm sitting next to the most beautiful woman in the world, my fiancée Laurin. (She's also a writer, so the clacking of the keyboards right now is deafening.) In just a few short weeks, she will become my bride. It seems God's goodness in my life knows no bounds.

I am beyond blessed, but not because I'm getting married. In fact, I considered not mentioning Laurin at all for fear the promise of the gospel might be reduced to a Hollywood happy ending. Jesus is good, and his love is unimaginably extravagant. But the Giver shouldn't be confused with his gifts. Whether my life is up or down, Jesus is enough. And that's why I wrote this book.

Endnotes

1.   "O LoveThatWill Not Let Me Go," lyrics by George Matheson (1882), music by Christopher Miner (1997)
2.   "The 'How' Matters;" sermon delivered by Matt Chandler atThe Village Church; Flower Mound,TX, 7/22/2012
3.   John Piper, *Future Grace*, (Sisters, OR; Multnomah Books) p 93
4.   C.S. Lewis, *The Weight of Glory*, (San Francisco, CA: HarperOne, 2009) p 86

bit.ly/OHeart

The Organized Heart
A Woman's Guide to Conquering Chaos

by Staci Eastin

Disorganized?
You don't need more rules, the latest technique, or a new gadget.

This book will show you a different, better way. A way grounded in the grace of God.

"Staci Eastin packs a gracious punch, full of insights about our disorganized hearts and lives, immediately followed by the balm of gospel-shaped hopes. This book is ideal for accountability partners and small groups."

> *Carolyn McCulley, blogger, filmmaker, author of* Radical Womanhood *and* Did I Kiss Marriage Goodbye?

"Unless we understand the spiritual dimension of productivity, our techniques will ultimately backfire. Find that dimension here. Encouraging and uplifting rather than guilt-driven, this book can help women who want to be more organized but know that adding a new method is not enough."

> *Matt Perman, Director of Strategy at Desiring God, blogger, author of the forthcoming book,* What's Best Next: How the Gospel Transforms the Way You Get Things Done

"Organizing a home can be an insurmountable challenge for a woman. The Organized Heart makes a unique connection between idols of the heart and the ability to run a well-managed home. This is not a how-to. Eastin looks at sin as the root problem of disorganization. She offers a fresh new approach and one I recommend, especially to those of us who have tried all the other self-help models and failed."

> *Aileen Challies, mom of three, and wife of blogger, author, and pastor Tim Challies*

The Organized Heart, by Staci Eastin

Excerpts from Chapter One: "Our Story"

Just two days before Christmas, and I was terribly behind.
We expected to leave town in thirty minutes and I had just started
packing. Todd, my husband, went to get gas, hoping that by dividing
the chores we could still get away on time. Meanwhile, I frantically dug through baskets of clean laundry, hoping to find enough
matching pairs of socks to see my preschool-age son through the
week. Each glance at the clock revealed that I would not finish in
time.

I began a mental list of all the reasons I wasn't ready. I don't
remember now what they were, but I'm sure I drew from the stock
of excuses I always used: unexpected events, needy children, unrea-
sonable demands from others. But as Todd returned, conviction
washed over me. None of my excuses were lies, but I wasn't being
completely honest. Because while my week had brought a few
surprises, I had still managed to find time for plenty of other things—
less important things.

When Todd returned home and walked into our bedroom, I
looked him in the eye and told him the truth. I was running late
because I hadn't prepared. It was all my fault.

....

I wish I could say that my story of holiday chaos was just
that—a season, and an unrepeated one—but I can't. One year later I
was running errands and half-listening to a Christian radio program
about New Year's Resolutions. Listeners called in and listed the
changes they wanted to make in the coming year: lose weight, quit
smoking, spend more time with their families. At each stoplight
I glanced at my to-do list, checking off anything recently accom-
plished, but also adding new tasks as they occurred to me. As the
uncompleted items piled up faster than the completed ones, I once
again felt the pressure of too much to do and too little time to do it in.
Suddenly I heard the host ask the radio audience to think of our own
resolutions, and I tearfully whispered, "I want to be more organized."

You may think I was being too hard on myself. Christmas is
a busy time, and it's only normal to feel stressed and rushed then.
But that season simply placed a spotlight on a constant reality.
My problem with disorganization seemed more apparent during

Christmas, but the problem was always there. In fact, my entire adult life could be described as a series of unfinished good intentions: notes and cards never sent (or even bought), dinner parties never thrown, kind words never spoken, calls never made, help never given.

So I come to you as someone who must fight to stay organized every day of her life.

In Pursuit of an Organized Home

My mother and my grandmothers were industrious women who showed me that organization is possible. They managed to keep clean houses, work, volunteer, and still have ample time for family, rest, and leisure. In an effort to be more like them, I have read countless books on home organization, and I own more planners than any person could ever need. I've tried lists, notebooks, note cards, and filing systems; I've posted schedules and spreadsheets; I've bought drawer organizers and closet systems. While all these things helped for a time, none brought the lasting change that I sought.

The systems, after all, require implementation, but my disorganized heart can corrupt a perfect rule and refuse a generous teacher. I can shove unfolded T-shirts into beautiful closet shelves or justify fudging on a sensible daily schedule. But the systems I tried don't get to the heart of why I do that. Most of these books and tools assume that disorganization stems from lack of skill. If I would just follow a certain system, I could enjoy a life of organized bliss. I could float through my spotless house, sail to all my appointments on time, and never feel stressed or rushed again.

....

I've come to see my disorganization as not due to a lack of skill or knowledge. I know how to keep a home, as I watched that done well all through my growing-up years. And since I already lacked the self-discipline to organize the tasks I knew needed doing anyway, the additional task of filling out a chart or planner just became one more thing to distract me from my priorities. Failing the system seemed inevitable.

....

So the real question is why I don't organize my days to do what I believe is important and what I do, in fact, have the skills and training to do. The answer is that I have a motivation problem. I do what I do not want to do—and I do not do what I want to do.

In Pursuit of an Organized Heart

Naturally organized people gain satisfaction from getting their work done quickly without procrastinating. They have learned to budget their time so that they don't take on more commitments than they can handle. They can easily whittle down their possessions to fit the amount of storage in their homes. When unexpected things come up, they prioritize between the urgent and non-urgent.

And then there is the rest of us. We know we shouldn't put required tasks off until the last minute, but something more pressing (or more fun) always seems to come up first. We know we shouldn't take on yet another commitment, but everything seems so important, and we don't want to let anyone down. Our closets, drawers, and garages overflow with extra stuff, but when we try to clean out, we can't part with any pieces. Some of us may even have spotless homes, but we're exhausted. We feel like we work all the time without any free time to relax and enjoy life the way other people do.

Secular psychologists tell us that we do these things because in our minds the payoff for disorganization is greater than the benefit of organization. We procrastinate because we don't want to do what needs to be done now. We overcommit because saying No hurts. We gain excess possessions because we prefer the certainty of having too much to the possibility of not having enough. We seek perfection because contentment feels like compromise. In other words, despite the fact that our lives are spinning out of control, in our twisted minds we believe that living this way is more pleasurable than taking steps to fix the problem.

I think those psychologists are partly right. The disorganization in my life was not due to lack of knowledge or skill and it was not due to a problem in my childhood. Rather, it's a broken belief system: a heart issue, a sin issue. At the end of the day, it's idolatry.

That may sound awfully harsh. You want this book to help you organize your life, not lay more guilt and shame at your feet. Being disorganized may be unhandy, but it's just your personality, right? It's certainly not a sin.

Or is it? Disorganization steals your joy. It causes you to go through your life frazzled and stressed. It causes friction with your husband and makes you snap at your children. It makes you perform ministry tasks grudgingly. It prevents you from developing friendships, because you're always rushing from one task to the next. You don't feel like you're doing anything well, let alone to the glory of God.

The Bible is clear that as Christians, we have tasks appointed to us by God (Ephesians 2:9-10). We should do everything we do with all our heart because we do it for the Lord (Colossians 3:23). As women, we are instructed to care for our homes and families (Titus 2:3-5). Whether we want to refer to our disorganization as personality quirks or sin, we must fight against anything that interferes with our relationship with God.

We never conquer sin by adding more rules. That's what the Pharisees did, and Jesus chastised them for it. Jesus is interested in more than just outward works; he wants us to perform good works from the overflow of a loving and pure heart. My attempts to get organized always failed because I tried to change my habits without letting the Holy Spirit change my heart. It was only when I saw the sinful motivations behind my bad habits that I could see lasting change in my life.

Starting to Start the Pursuit: Naming the Idols

This book will be different than any other book on organization that you've probably read. I have no schedule to offer you, I won't tell you what day to mop the kitchen floor, and you don't need to buy a timer. Your standards for an organized home and a reasonable schedule will vary with your personality, season of life, and the needs and preferences of your family.

What I hope to do is to help you examine your heart and discover things that may be hindering your walk with God. My goal is not necessarily for you to have a cleaner home or a more manageable schedule—although I certainly hope that is the case. Rather, my hope for this book is that it will help you serve God and your family more effectively, more fruitfully, and with greater peace and joy.

The Organized Heart *can be found at* **bit.ly/OHeart**

Who Am I?
Identity in Christ

by Jerry Bridges

Jerry Bridges unpacks Scripture to give the Christian eight clear, simple, interlocking answers to one of the most essential questions of life.

"Jerry Bridges' gift for simple but deep spiritual communication is fully displayed in this warm-hearted, biblical spelling out of the Christian's true identity in Christ."

J. I. Packer, Theological Editor, ESV Study Bible; author, Knowing God, A Quest for Godliness, Concise Theology

"I know of no one better prepared than Jerry Bridges to write *Who Am I?* He is a man who knows who he is in Christ and he helps us to see succinctly and clearly who we are to be. Thank you for another gift to the Church of your wisdom and insight in this book."

R.C. Sproul, founder, chairman, president, Ligonier Ministries; executive editor, Tabletalk magazine; general editor, The Reformation Study Bible

"*Who Am I?* answers one of the most pressing questions of our time in clear gospel categories straight from the Bible. This little book is a great resource to ground new believers and remind all of us of what God has made us through faith in Jesus. Thank the Lord for Jerry Bridges, who continues to provide the warm, clear, and biblically balanced teaching that has made him so beloved to this generation of Christians."

Richard D. Phillips, Senior Minister, Second Presbyterian Church, Greenville, SC

Who Am I? by Jerry Bridges

Excerpts from ChapterTwo: "I Am in Christ"

We have begun to answer the question "Who am I?" with the fact that we are all creatures, created in the image of God, dependent on him, and accountable to him. This is true of everyone born into the world whether we realize it or not. But for those of us who have trusted in Christ as our Savior, there is much more to our identity than simply being creatures.

The answer to the question, "Who am I as a Christian?", is far more elaborate and wonderful than the answer to the simpler (if still profound) question, "Who am I as a human being?" Once we are converted, there are seven additional glorious truths that come into play as essential components of our identity. These will constitute our focus for the remainder of this book.

As we seek to answer that more elaborate question, it is beyond dispute that we must start with the fact that we are "in" Christ Jesus.

What does it mean to be in Christ? Is it a question of location, like being in a house? Is it something like belonging to a club or an organization?

No, the term "in Christ" is the apostle Paul's shorthand expression for being united to Christ. It is one of Paul's favorite expressions, and (including similar expressions such as "in him" or "in the Lord") Paul uses it more than 160 times in his letters. Clearly this is an important concept in Paul's theology. And it should be an important concept for us because all the remaining answers to the question "Who am I?" are based upon the fact that we are in Christ, or we are united to Christ.

This of course begs the question, what does it mean to be united to Christ?

To answer it, we begin with 1 Corinthians 15:22, "For as in Adam all die, so also in Christ shall all be made alive." Note the two expressions "in Adam" and "in Christ." And again in 1 Corinthians 15:45, Paul refers to "the first man Adam" and to "the last Adam," who is clearly Christ. What Paul is getting at in these two verses is that in God's way of dealing with humanity there are only two men, Adam and Christ. All the rest of us are represented before God by one or the other of these two men.

Adam as Our Representative

In verse 22 Paul said, "in Adam all die." This idea is developed more completely in Romans 5:12-19. Verse 12 says, "Therefore, just as sin came into the world through one man, and death through sin, and so death spread to all men because all sinned…." This verse is a reference to Adam's sin of eating the forbidden fruit as recounted in Genesis 3. God had said, "but of the tree of the knowledge of good and evil you shall not eat, for in the day that you eat of it you shall surely die." Adam, along with Eve, ate, and they both died. They instantly died spiritually, and they would eventually die physically. But Adam was not an ordinary man so that the consequences of his sin would fall only on him.

Rather, Adam had been appointed by God to represent the entire human race. As a result, the consequences of his sin fell upon all humanity. When Paul writes in verse 12, "and so death spread to all men because all sinned…," he is referring, not to our own individual sins, but to the fact that we were so united to Adam as our representative head that when he sinned we all sinned, and so we all suffered the consequences of Adam's sin.

This idea of the representative nature of Adam's sin is further developed in verse 18, "Therefore, as one trespass led to condemnation for all men," and again in verse 19, "For as by the one man's disobedience the many were made sinners." Note especially in verse 19 the expression, "many were made sinners." All humanity (with the exception of Christ, who was not descended from Adam) suffered the consequences of Adam's sin. We were made sinners. As each of us comes into the world, we come as sinners by nature.

In answer to the question "Who am I?" we would therefore have to say, "I am a sinner." That is why David acknowledged, "Surely I was sinful at birth, sinful from the time my mother conceived me" (Psalms 51:5 NIV). David said the nature he received at conception was a sinful nature. Why was this true? It was because David, like you and me, was represented by Adam in the garden, and through the disobedience of Adam, David was made a sinner.

Picture two men, Adam and Christ, standing before God. Behind Adam stands all of humanity representatively united to him. We all come into this world "in Adam." Because of that, Paul's descriptive words in Ephesians 2:1-3 are true of every one of us before we trust Christ. Here is what he wrote:

And you were dead in the trespasses and sins in which you once walked, following the course of this world, following the prince of the power of the air, the spirit that is now at work in the sons of disobedience-- among whom we all once lived in the passions of our flesh, carrying out the desires of the body and the mind, and were by nature children of wrath, like the rest of mankind.

Paul's description of our dismal condition can be summed up in three expressions: "Spiritually dead," "Slaves" (to the world, the devil, and our sinful passions), and "Objects of God's wrath."

Think of that! As one "in Adam" you came into the world an object of God's wrath. It doesn't matter whether we were born of Christian parents or pagan parents. We are all born "in Adam" and so an object of God's wrath. All because Adam sinned.

Not only all of humanity, but creation itself suffered the consequences of Adam's sin. Though in Genesis 3:17-19, God refers specifically to cursing the ground, Paul in Romans 8:19-22, speaks of the futility of all creation. So we all come into the world spiritually dead, objects of God's wrath, and into a natural environment that is under the curse of God. That is what it means to be "in Adam."

Christ as Our Representative

The other man standing before God is the "last Adam," namely the Lord Jesus Christ. Just as God appointed Adam to represent all of humanity, so he appointed Christ to represent all who trust in him as Savior. We have looked at the consequences of Adam's representative act in Romans 5:18-19. Now observe the contrasting effects of Christ's work on behalf of all who trust in him. Verse 18: "so one act of righteousness leads to justification and life for all men." And in verse 19, "so by the one man's obedience the many will be made righteous."

For the sake of clarity, we need to draw out Paul's artful use of language in verses 18 and 19.

Verse 18: "as one trespass led to condemnation for all men, so one act of righteousness leads to justification and life for all men." In this verse, the first appearance of "all men" refers to our universal condemnation. The second appearance refers to the universal offer of salvation, not the universal existence of salvation. There is universal condemnation, and there is a universal way of escape, yet not all will escape.

Verse 19: "For as by the one man's disobedience the many were made sinners, so by the one man's obedience the many will be made righteous." Here, Paul follows the same artful use of language as in verse 18. The first appearance of "the many" is a universal statement, while the second appearance refers exclusively to those who come to Christ.

In each verse, therefore, the first "all" and "many" refer to the fact that all humanity has suffered the consequences of Adam's sin. The second "all" and "many" refer only to all those who trust in Christ and are "in him."

What are the results of being in him? We will explore these in detail in subsequent chapters, but for now I want to call our attention to the principle by which God operates.

Obedience and Disobedience

In Deuteronomy 28, Moses sets before the nation of Israel two alternatives: obedience and disobedience. The results of obedience are tremendous blessings. The results of disobedience are horrible curses. These particular blessings and curses are all temporal in nature and refer specifically to Israel in the Promised Land. But at the same time they are an expression of the eternal principle by which God operates: blessings for obedience, and curses for disobedience.

By his perfectly obedient life over 33 years, Christ earned the blessings of God. By his death on the cross he experienced the curse for disobedience. As our representative, all that he did in both his life and death accrues to our benefit. Someone has said it like this: "He lived the life we could not live, and died the death we deserved to die." Or again, "He was treated as we deserved to be treated in order that we might be treated as he deserved to be treated."

When we think of the work of Christ, we usually think of his death to pay for our sin. We call this his "substitutionary atonement," in that he died in our place, as our substitute, to satisfy the justice of God for our sins. But what is it that makes this substitution valid? How could God's justice be satisfied when a perfectly innocent man suffers punishment on behalf of those who actually deserve it?

The answer is that Christ stood before God as our representative. He assumed the responsibility for our obedience to the law of God, and he assumed the responsibility to render to God satisfaction for our disobedience. All this because we are "in him," that is, we are united to him in a representative way.

bit.ly/Christ-in

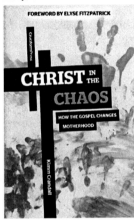

Christ in the Chaos
How the Gospel Changes Motherhood

by Kimm Crandall

MOMS: Stop comparing yourself to others. Stop striving to meet false expectations. Stop thinking your performance dictates your worth.

Look to the gospel for rest, joy, sufficiency, identity, and motivation.

"Although Kimm Crandall's message would revive any soul longing for the breath of the gospel of grace, I am especially eager to recommend this book to that heart who strives to know God and to make him known to the little ones who call her 'Momma.' Kimm is a candid and gracious fellow sojourner, faithfully pointing to God's immeasurable steadfast love and grace in the midst of our mess."

> *Lauren Chandler, wife of Matt Chandler (pastor of The Village Church), mother of three, writer, singer, and speaker*

"What an amazingly wild and wise, disruptive and delighting, freeing and focusing book. Kimm's book is for every parent willing to take the stewardship of children and the riches of the gospel seriously. This is one of the most helpful and encouraging books on parenting I've read in the past twenty years. This will be a book you will want to give to parents, to-be parents, and grandparents."

> *Scotty Smith, author; Founding Pastor, Christ Community Church*

"Kimm Crandall has discovered that chaos can be the perfect context in which to experience God's liberating grace. She is a wise, practical, gospel-drenched guide for anyone navigating through the wearisome terrain of parenting."

> *Tullian Tchividjian, author; Pastor, Coral Ridge Presbyterian Church*

bit.ly/CPModest

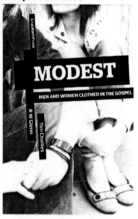

Modest
Men and Women Clothed in the Gospel

by R W Glenn, Tim Challies

Modesty is about freedom, not rules.

What you say or do or wear is not really the point. The point is your heart.

True modesty flows from a solid grasp of the gospel.

"It is so refreshing to have a book on modesty that is a useful resource and not a legalistic, culture-bound list that leaves you a bit paranoid and guilty. No, this book is different. Its counsel on modesty is not rooted in rules, but in the grace of the gospel of Jesus Christ. That grace alone is able to get at the heart of the problem of modesty, which *is* the heart. In a culture where immodesty is the accepted norm, Glenn and Challies have given us help that every Christian desperately needs."

Paul Tripp, pastor, conference speaker, and author

"How short is too short? How tight is too tight? Glenn and Challies don't say. But they do provide a thoughtful framework to help us come to a grace-based, gospel-grounded understanding of modesty that extends beyond mere clothing. They uphold a vision for modesty that's both beautiful and desirable – and not only for gals, but for guys too! This book is a great tool to help you wrestle with the practical question of what and what not to wear."

Mary A. Kassian, Author, Girls Gone Wise

"The authors of Modest break new ground in their treatment of this difficult subject. It is a healthy antidote to the prevailing views, which tend toward either legalism or antinomianism, by grounding the whole subject in the gospel. I heartily recommend this book."

Jerry Bridges, Author, The Pursuit of Holiness

bit.ly/IParent

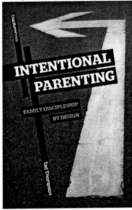

Intentional Parenting
Family Discipleship by Design

by Tad Thompson

**The Big Picture and a Simple Plan —
That's What You Need to Do Family
Discipleship Well**

*This book will allow you to take all the
sermons, teachings, and exhortations
you have received on the topic of
family discipleship, make sense of it,
and put it to use.*

"As parents, we know God has given us the responsibility to train our
children in his ways. But many parents don't know where or how to
start. Tad has done us all a favor by identifying seven key categories
of biblical teaching we can utilize in teaching our children godly
truth and principles. This easy-to-follow plan will help any parent
put the truth of God's Word into their children's hearts."
Kevin Ezell, President, North American Mission Board,
Southern Baptist Convention; father of six

"Here is a practical page-turner that encourages fathers to engage the
hearts of their families with truth and grace. In an age when truth is
either ignored or despised, it is refreshing to see a book written for
ordinary fathers who want their families to be sanctified by the truth.
Thompson writes with a grace which reminds us that parenting
flows from the sweet mercies of Christ."
Joel Beeke, President, Puritan Reformed Theological
Seminary

"Need an introductory text to the topic of discipling children? Here is
a clear, simple book on family discipleship, centered on the gospel
rather than human successes or external behaviors."
James M. Hamilton, Associate Professor of Biblical
Theology, The Southern Baptist Theological Seminary

The Two Fears
Tremble Before God Alone

by Chris Poblete

**You can fear God...
or everything else.**

**Only one fear brings life and hope,
wisdom and joy.**

Fear wisely.

"We are too scared. And we aren't scared enough. Reading this book
   will prompt you to seek in your own life the biblical tension between
   'fear not' and 'fear God.'"
   ### *Russell D. Moore, Dean, Southern Baptist Theological Seminary*

"An importantly counter-cultural book, moving us beyond a
   homeboy God we could fist-bump to a holy God we can worship.
   The Two Fears helps us recover a biblical fear of God and all the awe,
   repentance, and freedom from self-centered fears that go with it. An
   awesome resource!"
   ### *Dr. Thaddeus Williams, professor, Biola University*

"In this practical and very readable book, Chris Poblete shows how
   both the absence of true fear and the presence of 'unholy [false] fear'
   stem from an absence of a knowledge of the awesome God of the
   Bible, and that, in meeting him, we discover the real dimensions of
   creational existence and the wonderful benefits of living in fear and
   deep respect before him, freed from the '[false] fear of men.'"
   ### *Peter Jones, Ph.D., TruthXchange; Scholar-in-Residence and
   Adjunct Professor, Westminster Seminary in California*

"I commend this book to you: it will fuel your worship and empower
   your discipleship."
   ### *Gabe Tribbett, Christ's Covenant Church, Winona Lake, IA*

CPSIA information can be obtained at www.ICGtesting.com
Printed in the USA
LVOW10s1025060913

351175LV00015B/246/P